SACK THE BOARD!

Allan Caldwell was born in Glasgow. He began his career in journalism on local newspapers and spent two years studying journalism at Napier University before turning freelance. He then worked with Radio Clyde in Glasgow before joining the BBC as a radio reporter then on television covering news and sport. After seven years he moved to Sky Television before returning to newspapers and is currently a freelance journalist based in Glasgow.

Allan Caldwell covered the Celtic story for the *Evening Times*. The exclusive revelations contained in his reports – regarding the directors' secret pact, the transatlantic faxes and the foreign bank which denied having put up money – were partly responsible for the downfall of the Celtic board.

SACK THE BOARD!

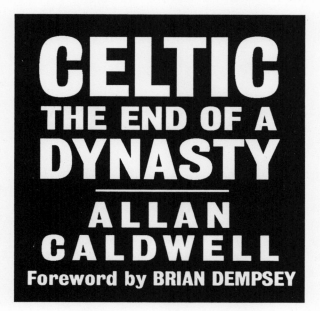

CELTIC
THE END OF A
DYNASTY

ALLAN CALDWELL

Foreword by BRIAN DEMPSEY

MAINSTREAM
PUBLISHING

EDINBURGH AND LONDON

First published in Great Britain in 1994 by
MAINSTREAM PUBLISHING COMPANY (EDINBURGH) LTD
7 Albany Street
Edinburgh EH1 3UG

ISBN 1 85158 682 2

A catalogue record for this book is available from the British
Library

Typeset in Palatino by Litho Link Ltd., Welshpool, Powys
Printed in Great Britain by Butler & Tanner Ltd, Frome

Contents

Foreword
by Brian Dempsey

OVER the past three years Allan Caldwell has covered most of what has transpired at Celtic Football Club. To say that I have been deeply involved in matters is an understatement. I commend this fully independent assertion of events as they unfolded since the day my ratification as a director was lost. The author has been in touch with me constantly throughout and after the battle but this is not my story.

I have not had the luxury of editing anything which has been written for this book and, indeed, have not read what comments of mine are to be included. However, I have respect for the author and believe Celtic needs a meticulously documented account of what has transpired. This will give Celtic supporters and football supporters in general the facility to read how an institution like Celtic set off towards the rocks and ended up at its favoured destination.

It is important, if not critical, that the final downfall of the Celtic board came just days after Allan Caldwell's report that the merchant bank Gefinor did not have the agreement with Celtic over the Cambuslang stadium project as was announced at the time. That led to a final vote of no confidence in the Celtic board from the supporters, the shareholders and ultimately the bank.

Allan Caldwell and I may not agree on everything reported during the struggle of the last three or more years but, what is important, is that the facts speak for themselves.

Read and be informed.

Prologue

Euphoria

Friday, 4 March 1994, 2.15 pm.

THEY SANG. They danced. They laughed and they cried.

The steps leading to the red-faced, brick frontage at the Parkhead stadium were awash with joyful fans. A cold wind swept over the two hundred or so who had earlier huddled together in a group awaiting the news. But nothing, not even the worst of the elements Mother Nature could throw at them, would stop the celebration.

There had never been scenes like it at Celtic Park for many, many years . . . not since captain Billy McNeill had held aloft the European Cup nearly 27 years earlier. This was the moment to savour. One the supporters had been waiting for throughout more than three long and miserable years.

The sun broke for the first time through the grey, threatening clouds as the 'saviours' arrived at the historic Glasgow club. 'Hail, hail the Celts are here!' was the cry as city businessman Brian Dempsey and Canadian-based millionaire Fergus McCann were swept through the crowd to the front entrance.

Fergus McCann for once looked humbled. The bespectacled, unassuming tycoon wore a cloth cap which looked completely out of place against his camel hair coat and silk tie. He was almost lost alongside the taller, broader and brighter figure of Dempsey. But it wasn't long before the smile reappeared below his neatly trimmed moustache.

It was a personal triumph for both and the end to a long and bloody battle for control of a club they *both* so dearly loved and hated to see being destroyed. Cheers and applause now followed as the two ignored the chill wind and beamed with delight to the flash of cameras and the cheers and applause of ecstatic fans.

'Who owns the club now?' It was a voice from somewhere among the mass of bodies cramming even closer to their new leaders.

Brian Dempsey poked himself on the chest and shouted: 'We do! The game is over. The rebels have won.'

It was what the supporters wanted to hear. Music to their ears. Tough talking was still to be done to formally complete the deal but it was effectively over. Out were hated directors Chris White, Michael Kelly and David Smith. It also meant an end to the family dynasties the Whites and Kellys had held over the club for 106 years.

The chants grew louder: 'The board is dead . . . long live the board.'

A new era was dawning.

Chapter One

The Last Supper

Three-and-a-half years earlier.
Thursday, 25 October 1990, 11 p.m.

'I REMEMBER that night well. There had been rumblings but nothing to suggest what was about to unfold.' *Brian Dempsey*.

CELTIC director Brian Dempsey flopped into his hotel bed.

It had been a long and hard day's business and Manchester was not his favourite place. Now his cold was getting worse. Beads of sweat broke from his forehead and his head began to thump. Sleeping would not be an easy task tonight.

It had been a tiring six months. Keeping a tight rein on a busy building and property development company and trying to cure the ills of Celtic Football Club was quite a juggling act.

His appointment at Parkhead back on 3 May was quite sudden but very gratifying. Along with former Glasgow Lord Provost Michael Kelly the pledges were made: 'We'll stick together on this one and pull Celtic into the 21st century.' Kelly was now in the public relations business – just what Celtic needed.

It was always going to be a struggle but things were looking good. Land purchased at Robroyston in the north of Glasgow by the Dempsey firm Strathvale was on offer to the club as the site for a new stadium. Celtic had to put up only £1.2 million for a quarter share in the site and surrounding land. Planning permission was there in principle for further developments, including an hotel and service station. Celtic's share from the sale of the surrounding land would be likely to yield £10 million – practically all they would need to build the new stadium. The rest of the cash would come from grants and sponsors.

But Celtic directors Chris White and Michael Kelly were uneasy. They didn't like the plan. Dempsey had been trying to win them over but they seemed entrenched in the narrow-mindedness which was becoming a Celtic trait with the new breed of family dynasties Kelly and White had brought to the club.

The Government's Taylor Report imposing all-seated stadium legislation by 1994 had brought a sense of urgency to the need for change and investment. Cash also had to be raised and the best way for that to happen was to turn this private family firm into a public company which would also let the fans have a say in the club they loved. The White and Kelly faction did not seem to realise this need for quick decisions. In fact, the ostrich syndrome appeared to have set in. Their heads were buried deep in the sand. They were oblivious to the tough talking and the frequent kicks on the backside. 'Ignore it and it will go away' seemed to be their view.

Ignore it and it will go away. The words were repeated by Dempsey as the sweat soaked the pillow. But it didn't go away. The headache and the pained limbs were getting worse. There was no point in kidding on. At the age of 42, with the stress and pressures abounding and little exercise, this was no time for heroics. The meetings the following day were cancelled and the Dempsey home in the comfortable Glasgow suburb of Millngavie beckoned.

The Skol Cup final against Rangers was two days away. A glorious Sunday outing to Hampden Park for which he wanted to feel better. A wife, two daughters and a son were more than capable of ensuring he stayed in bed for a few days of recovery.

Or so he thought.

The telephone call from chairman Jack McGinn was insistent. 'You have to attend the annual general meeting tonight.'

Okay, thought Dempsey. They have to ratify my position as a director and I suppose I should be there. He hauled himself from his sickbed, showered, dressed quickly and accepted the offer of a lift to Parkhead. His head was still thumping and his temperature was getting higher by the hour. But needs be.

It was the usual routine before an AGM. A meal in the Walfrid restaurant at Celtic Park before heading through to the Jock Stein lounge for the shareholders meeting.

All of the directors were there . . . Chairman Jack McGinn, largest shareholder and youngest board member Chris White, Michael Kelly, his cousin Kevin, lawyer Jimmy Farrell and stadium manager 'caretaker' Tom Grant. The meal was pleasant enough as was the wine and the chat. They all sat together enjoying their supper with little hint of what was to follow.

Dempsey sipped a cup of coffee hoping to clear his head, unaware there was a Judas beside him. The pieces of silver must have been rattling as the seven rose and headed for the Jock Stein lounge.

It was Michael Kelly who spoke the words. 'Chris White and I are going to oppose your ratification as a director.'

Dempsey stopped in his tracks and stared at him. He couldn't believe the words just uttered. They hit him like a glacier. There was little that could be done. No time. The AGM was about to start. The timing had been immaculate.

Ten minutes later the meeting began and soon Brian Dempsey was no longer a director of Celtic Football Club.

He had said little to the astounded media pack as he made his way out of Celtic Park. Numb with cold. Numb with shock. It was a freezing, damp and frosty night. He climbed into the waiting car and headed home. Reality had not quite sunk in. Perhaps if he laid his head back on his pillow he would awake and discover the whole night had been nothing more than a bad dream.

The calls from the media in the morning confirmed it was a real nightmare.

It has been a carefully orchestrated manoeuvre. The unholy White-Kelly alliance had gathered enough support from the floor of the meeting to have their motion passed. It had seemed incredible. Even the other directors were shocked. They were behind Dempsey but didn't have enough voting clout to stop his removal. The meeting had at first confirmed his appointment on a show of hands but a ballot was insisted on by the devious duo of directors. This was based on the number of shares held by individuals and it was obvious the two had already secured enough votes from family and friends holding large numbers of shares.

Newspaper headlines that morning summed up the events of the previous evening . . . 'Celts in Turmoil', 'Night of the Long Knives'. Chairman Jack McGinn was quoted as saying: 'I am disappointed to lose Brian because I think he had a great deal to offer this club.' Longest-serving director Jimmy Farrell described the sacking of Dempsey as 'a real tragedy for Celtic'. He added: 'I am totally shocked and disappointed. I had no inkling that this would happen. Celtic have never acted like this in my time here.'

White and public relations boss Kelly were unrepentant. They refused to speak personally. Through a spokesman they issued a statement saying: 'We have been concerned for some time that while we have been spending all our time planning how to spend millions of pounds on a new or refurbished stadium we have ignored the most important requirement. What we need to do is improve our profitability and show how we can raise funds through our own commercial operations.' The spokesman refused to say why Dempsey was ousted but said it was unlikely any plans for Celtic becoming a public company would go ahead.

Dempsey then read his own comments printed in the *Evening Times*. The story was critical of the move by Kelly and White. It said Dempsey himself refused to get embroiled in a war of words and quoted the millionaire building magnate as saying: 'The important matter for the club this weekend is not what happens to me but what takes place tomorrow at Hampden.'

Dempsey described that night as one of the worst in his life. He recalled: 'When I arrived for the supper Chris White and Michael Kelly were not there. They were "talking" in another room. I asked Tom Grant to go and ask them what was keeping them. Tom said when he walked into the room and disturbed them you would have thought someone had just thrown a hand grenade inside.

'They came through and said nothing. We ate and when Michael Kelly then told me he and White were not going to ratify my position as director I was stunned. I told him not to do that on the eve of a cup final and even offered to write a quick letter of resignation which they could announce after the final. Michael Kelly refused and said it was something they must do. Those words still haunt me.

'It was a public humiliation which was what they were trying to achieve. It has a damaging effect on you especially when in business and dealing with banks. It is as if people have no confidence in you and for a while I found myself defending everything I did and said – even in front of my friends.

'Billy McNeill called me just after midnight when he heard the news and asked what he should tell the players, who would read about it on the morning of the final. I simply told him to tell the players the truth. Billy was shattered. The players had warmed to me thinking change was on the way at Parkhead. It was sad but there was nothing I could do.'

The following day Dempsey, a little more refreshed and a little less numb, headed for Hampden for the cup final. Thoughts of his removal were pushed to the back of a tired mind. Football, after all, is what the game is all about. Instead of taking a seat in the directors' box, as was planned only two days before, he joined other Celtic supporters in the stand.

The events of the last 48 hours were not the best in terms of preparation for the team led by manager and former captain Billy McNeill. They lost. Old Firm rivals Rangers won 2–1 . . . a result which merely added to the bitter taste in the mouths of many.

Monday's press included as much coverage of the AGM fiasco as there was of the match. 'The Way Ahead' and 'Celtic hope to cash in with executive signing' were two headlines reporting attempts by director Chris White to retain some form of credibility over the mess he and his cohort Michael Kelly now found themselves in.

White – son of the late club chairman Desmond – had been somewhat taken aback by the ferocity of the criticism fired at him. He was not the best judge of character and did not appear to appreciate the support Dempsey had. But, with the advice of Michael Kelly, he had come up with a new plan to deflect the scathing words heading their way. It was simple . . . appoint a chief executive and have the media fill their minds with that and the controversial scenarios that came with such a new and bold initiative.

White and Kelly were quite smug with themselves. It had worked to an extent. But while the media deliberated over this new distraction, the White and Kelly team were at it again. Chris White sat in his office and must have felt quite content. His quotes made good reading – to him. Particularly the lines: 'First and foremost we must restore unity on the board. What has happened is not the Celtic way of working. We must all get together and work for what I see as an exciting future for the club. The moves I instigated were not taken lightly but were moves that I felt had to be taken for the good of the club.'

What the press were not aware of was the call he had just made to director Jimmy Farrell. White and Michael Kelly were not at all happy with the comments the senior board member had made after the AGM. How dare he criticise them and support Dempsey? White had just asked Farrell to resign. His only crime appeared to have been the comments he had made.

But it was White who was not happy now. Farrell would not be bullied and had refused to bow to the request to quit.

Chairman Jack McGinn had also shown his support for Dempsey. The split on the board had appeared. And it was growing quickly.

Dempsey now decided it was time to take a back seat. He needed time for his wounds to heal. There was business to be done and Christmas was fast approaching. Not the time for bitterness.

But he did allow himself a little chuckle. The media were beginning to scrutinise the actions of Kelly and White and the plans for the future of the club. Plans which now lay in tatters. Even with a chief executive major decisions would have to be made by the board and they would have to be made fast. Celtic were falling behind their greatest rivals, Rangers, whose Ibrox stadium was rising like a jewel in the football crown. Questions were also being asked about the family traditions at Celtic and the control the Whites and Kellys had over the club. Change was in the air, thought Dempsey. It might be a long time coming but it would happen.

The first change was quick but expected – a new chief executive, as promised by White. Terry Cassidy, a former newspaper executive, was, according to White, worth the £60,000 a year salary and was the right man for the job. White told the media: 'We set out to find the best person and we have. He has all the qualities to release the full potential of Celtic as a force in modern football.'

Englishman Cassidy revealed one of his qualities when he announced: 'I am not a Celtic fan. But I have been impressed with the directors. Everyone is pulling in the same direction, the atmosphere at this club is good.'

Dempsey liked that. It appealed to his sense of humour even if Cassidy was trying to be sincere.

Christmas came and went. So too did New Year and another defeat at the hands of Rangers. So too did the discussions and the arguments over Celtic. The team were not doing well and there were suggestions Billy McNeill could be for the chop. The first hint of rebellion from the fans was scented. Executive box members – many of whom supported Dempsey – were putting the blame for the club's ills squarely at the feet of the directors.

Cassidy hit out at the 18 executive fans who threatened to withdraw their £250,000 support for the club. He warned: 'As sure as night follows day, Celtic will be back on top. And these same people might find it difficult to get back in.'

Dempsey was back behind his desk when the call came out of the blue. It was Cassidy. A meeting? It was certainly intriguing, thought Dempsey, so he agreed.

Cassidy said at the time: 'If there is anyone who can do anything to help get this club back to where they should be,

I want to meet them. I want to assess for myself if there is anything Brian Dempsey can offer the club. If there is, and if he agrees, I will ask for his support. And I would expect the full backing of the board. If the board rejected my proposals then they would have to give me good reason.'

Dempsey decided to add a little spice to it all by throwing in his own comment: 'I will meet Mr Cassidy . . . as a matter of courtesy.'

Cassidy was quick into print again with an interview to the *Scotland on Sunday*. This time he pushed it too far. He stated: 'Mr Dempsey is going to have to do a lot of talking to convince me he is interested in Celtic's good health. If he is, it seems to me that he should be unequivocally denouncing some of the things that are appearing in the papers.'

Dempsey didn't like those comments. What things? Legal action was threatened. The so-called 'peace meeting' between the two was now squaring up to be a full-blown boxing match.

However, Dempsey decided to meet the man for himself. But it would be on his ground. No way, he thought, would he go to Parkhead for such a confrontation. Cassidy duly turned up for the meeting at Dempsey's office on 8 January. But he was not happy with the reception. 'The place,' he recalled, 'was full of journalists. Brian Dempsey had asked for the meeting to be kept secret and I agreed to that but when I turned up at his office it was packed with journalists. I asked him where they all came from and he said, "I don't know. I was going to ask you the same question."'

The meeting lasted an hour. There was not much to it – as expected. Cassidy emerged full of smiles and said he was glad he had learned first hand of Dempsey's plan for a new stadium at Robroyston. It was Cassidy who had to whittle down the various options which also included redeveloping Parkhead.

Dempsey was glad he had set the record straight with Cassidy and that he had done so forcibly.

Cassidy rubbed his hands. A good day done. In the few weeks he had been at the club he had achieved quite a bit. He had fallen out with the media after accusing them of 'putting the boot into Celtic', he had upset Dempsey and effectively dismissed the executive box holders. Good start, thought Dempsey.

Cassidy's view of events was slightly different. He believed he was there to take the flak for the directors and to protect the club and its employees. He had little respect for journalists and was of the opinion they would write what they wanted no matter the facts as he saw them.

But he would have to live with Dempsey for a while yet. It had been three months now since Dempsey was unceremoniously removed as a director. Time had healed the wounds. Well, most of them. There was still one festering away and it was known collectively as Kelly and White. Dempsey had already decided they were not good for Celtic Football Club and the first move in the rebellion was about to be made.

It was a quiet and low-key sortie. A probe at the defences of the enemy. There was a Kelly who would sell his shares. The family link in question was James G. Kelly jnr who lived in California. He was the grandnephew of the late Celtic chairman Sir Robert Kelly and he was prepared to part with 120 shares. But he wanted £167 for each of his £3.50 shares.

Edinburgh businessman John Keane took up the offer and paid out £20,000. Then he sat back and waited. Under Celtic's private company and family dynasty rules, no-one could sell or buy shares without the approval of the board. The transfer request was quickly spotted – and blocked. A fuming Terry Cassidy was wheeled out by the board to publicly lambast Keane. He blasted: 'Why do things like this always have to become public property and an embarrassment to Celtic? We were never told officially about the deal, simply tipped off. The board discussed the matter and decided they were unhappy about the manner in which this transaction was conducted.

'If there is some sort of attempt here to break the Celtic Park dynasties I would say this is the wrong way to go about it. Why didn't Mr Keane approach myself or a club director in confidence and let it be known he was considering such a move?'

The answer to that was simple and the board knew it. John Keane was Brian Dempsey's business partner.

Dempsey made another, more subtle, move. He bought a 75 per cent stake in Harry Hynds Travel. It was the agency which arranged most of Celtic's trips to Europe and those for the fans.

Meanwhile Chris White and Michael Kelly were quietly drawing up their own plans but theirs were plans of defence. They were not in a position to attack. Cassidy's knack of causing controversy was drawing attention away from them. He was taking the flak and they needed that. But on the park the team were struggling. Badly. The other members of the board were becoming increasingly suspicious of the White and Kelly alliance. Rumblings were being heard. That was also a threat. Then there were the fans.

'The fans'. Many believed there were times when Chris White hated the fans. A group had broken away from the official supporters' association and called themselves Save Our Celts. They held an inaugural meeting on 25 February. It was a sunny but bitterly cold day. Around 500 trekked along to the Shettleston Hall. Dempsey had thought long and hard about accepting the invitation to attend as a guest speaker. But he decided it was time to be seen in the fight, leading his troops from the front. Only directors Jimmy Farrell – a Dempsey supporter – and Tom Grant accepted similar invitations.

According to the chairman of the meeting, criminal lawyer Joe Beltrami, Chris White had declared the rally would 'serve little purpose and simply cause embarrassment to the club'. At least he got the last part right.

Dempsey rose to his feet to the cheers of the supporters and immediately appealed to the board: 'For God's sake, stop this childish petulance – that if anyone dares to criticise he is creating mischief. Stop the paranoia – that if anyone dares to ask a question he is causing embarrassment. We are not. Celtic is a love affair that we take to our deaths.'

If that wasn't bad enough for the board worse was quick to follow. Now the executive box holders had formed a club – the Celtic Fair Weather Supporters. The name came from a comment by Cassidy referring to the disgruntled executive box holders. They had just sponsored an away match at Dunfermline claiming their £2,000 cash was better off with another outfit. For their money they were entertained by the Dunfermline officials and given seats in the same directors' box as the visiting Celtic directors. It was also announced over the loudspeaker system several times that the match was being sponsored by Celtic fans. That confused the Fifers' home support and deeply embarrassed the Celtic directors.

Leader of the group was one Harry Hynds.

It didn't take long for the directors to put two and two together. Two weeks after the Dunfermline game Cassidy issued an internal memo to staff at Celtic Park. 'Do not use Harry Hynds Travel' was the message. It informed officials the agency had been dropped and the contract placed with a rival firm.

Cassidy appeared quite smug with himself as he announced the decision. He said: 'Some people seem to think they can embarrass Celtic Football Club in public and no-one will do anything about it. That is silly. We will fight it. I don't want to lose any sponsor, every one is important to this club. However, we have to stress no individual is bigger than Celtic Football Club.'

Dempsey sat back in his chair. He mused over the comments. Thoughts now wandered to the next move in this skirmish with Cassidy. He was proving to be a worthy adversary but he frequently left himself exposed. Dempsey would always be able to strike at such times if he so desired.

The real danger, he knew, lay with Chris White and Michael Kelly. They had now struck up a strong though questionable bond. Their grip was getting stronger and had to be weakened before it was too late.

Cassidy meanwhile was off on another quest – the quest for the great Celtic stadium. He and the board had still to make up their minds on which of several sites to choose from.

By now they had concluded an alternative site to Parkhead had to be identified, although the option of a revamped Celtic Park was still there. A consortium had been hired to consult the club on the choice and the way forward. London-based Superstadia had arrived on the scene. Cassidy revealed the choices as the redevelopment of Celtic Park, ground-sharing at the national stadium – Hampden – or one of two sites outwith Parkhead which he refused to identify.

Cassidy said: 'Ideally the new ground would be multi-purpose and available for use on any day of the year and for most events. The heart says we should continue where we are, but I'm not sure we could achieve what we would like here. I'd like Celtic to be the club which builds THE stadium, THE arena, in the country.'

Trouble is, wondered Dempsey, the team is not the team it should be and certainly not the team needed to fill such a great stadium should it ever happen. On that front Cassidy was at pains to dispel rumours that the job of

Celtic manager Billy McNeill was under threat. He said: 'I have asked Billy to tell me what salary and benefits he believes the manager of Celtic should be given.' In fact Cassidy had asked all senior executives at the club to justify their position and salary. 'If Billy does not provide the information I have requested in time, then he'll get whatever I give him.'

There was just one small, fundamental flaw. Cassidy was already aware of a secret document drawn up on how to handle the sacking of Billy McNeill. And that bombshell was about to be publicly dropped in an affair which was to prove one of the most shameful in the history of Celtic Football Club.

Trouble was, Cassidy and the directors did not know what was about to hit them.

Chapter Two

Find the Mole

Friday, 10 May 1991, 1 pm.

IT was a typical Friday afternoon in the Scottish newsroom at the *Sun*. There was plenty of news about and good enough tales coming up from down south to make a decent front page splash story. But Crawford Brankin much preferred a good Scottish exclusive. Brankin was the tabloid's deputy editor and news editor. He regarded the motivation of his staff as part of his job and he presently had them chasing around for a good story.

It did look though as if they would draw a blank today. It was the eve of the big game. Rangers playing Aberdeen tomorrow with the league title within their grasp. Celtic were well out of contention and there were more rumours and counter-rumours about the future of Billy McNeill as manager. But no-one believed Celtic would consider firing the hero of the Lisbon Lions, the captain of the first British team to lift the European Cup in 1967.

Not after the last fall-out. That had happened almost eight years ago when McNeill enjoyed a five-year successful spell as Celtic manager. He left then to go south after a personality clash with the late chairman, Desmond White, and a salary dispute.

Brankin's phone shrieked at him again. Either another correspondent or another complaint, he thought. It was a freelance journalist. One he knew well . . . and trusted. But what he was claiming seemed too good to be true.

'Okay,' said Brankin. 'I'll meet you in the usual haunt. I'll take the tube 'cause the city's too busy and I'll never get parked there.' He said nothing to the others, put his jacket on and walked out of the *Sun* building in Kinning Park. The underground was just around the corner and it would soon whisk him below the River Clyde and into Queen Street station in the city centre.

The bar was close by. It was a pleasant enough place although a bit dimly lit for Brankin's taste. Ideal though for these sort of meetings.

His contact was already at the bar, a glass of dry white wine in his hand. Soon they were sitting at a table in the corner. The document was passed across and Brankin read it.

'How confident are you this is genuine?' he asked.

'Very confident. My source has never let me down before,' was the reply.

Brankin liked what he heard and loved what he saw. The document had been drawn up in memo form by Terry Cassidy. It concerned the future of manager Billy McNeill and there were no two questions about it. This document pointed heavily to his sacking and detailed how the club would handle it. There was even a draft press release to announce the news. Brankin thought to himself for a moment. If it was genuine, this was dynamite.

As the 'clockwork orange' rumbled back towards Kinning Park underground station Brankin read the memo again. The more he read it the more he believed it. By the time he reached his office he was convinced.

Convincing the others in the newsroom was not too difficult. His enthusiasm overcame their scepticism and soon two reporters were phoning furiously around trying to find the Celtic directors.

By the time they had finished they were even more convinced. Some had denied any knowledge of the memo, others made no comment but Terry Cassidy had spoken at length. He had been very evasive and would not deny the document existed. His signature at the bottom of the document had been checked against a known original. It matched.

Brankin decided the story would run but the exact details contained in the memo would not be reprinted just yet. 'Celtic's Secret Plan to Sack Billy' was the front page headline in the paper the next morning. It had tremendous effect, as Brankin knew it would. The directors were now under fire from the rest of the Scottish media to comment on the story. 'Was it true?' they asked. 'No comment' was the usual reply.

But such was the pressure on the directors that Terry Cassidy did comment. He was still being evasive and still refused to confirm or deny the existence of the document. But he did say in reply to questions from Alan Davidson in the Saturday *Evening Times*: 'It is unthinkable that someone on the board of directors should leak a confidential document. If that is the case then there is only one course of action that can possibly follow.'

The article went under the heading: 'MOLE HUNT. Sack threat after 'axe McNeill' leak'. It stated Cassidy was ready to launch a hunt for the 'mole' who leaked the secret document. The article concluded from Cassidy's comments that only the six directors – Jack McGinn, Chris White, Jimmy Farrell, Kevin Kelly, Tom Grant and Michael Kelly – had seen and possessed copies of the memo. The leaked document had to have come from one of them.

Cassidy then said on television the next day: 'If the *Sun* has the document then let them run it.' That was all Brankin needed to hear. On the Monday the paper ran another front page story and this time carried most of the seven major points of the memo word for word.

The confidential blueprint proposed that any change of manager must be handled professionally to protect the dignity and pride of everyone involved. It also suggested the release of an agreed press statement and a scenario in which assistant boss Tommy Craig would become caretaker manager and a candidate for McNeill's job.

The story infuriated Cassidy and the Celtic directors. The hunt for the 'mole' intensified.

Brian Dempsey was equally infuriated. He had a lot of respect for Billy McNeill and was outraged the directors should treat one of their greatest players this way. The feelings were echoed by the fans but nothing was being said at Parkhead.

McNeill himself was clearly angry at the way Cassidy and the directors were behaving. He had lived with the constant rumours for months. Now the crunch had come and he wanted to know where he stood. He said: 'Now is the time for the board of directors to make their comments on any decision that has been made. That is all I can say on the matter – for the present.'

Although maintaining a dignified stance on the subject, McNeill was seething. As one of the club's most faithful servants, McNeill believed, indeed expected, he should receive better treatment at the hands of those who governed at Celtic Park. But nothing was forthcoming from the Silent Six. The directors were shying away from the glare of publicity surrounding them.

The days passed and still nothing but Press speculation. The public spit-roasting of Billy McNeill, MBE, was a disgrace. For 22 years he had been an inspiration on the field for Celtic, having arrived at the Parkhead club as a boy in 1957. Under his captaincy Celtic became the first British club to win the European Cup. Also during his long spell as captain the team had won the League Championship nine times, six times had their hands on the Scottish Cup and the League Cup five times.

Ten more days passed with the bungling board still to make up their minds. McNeill hid well his frustration and fury. But deep inside he knew the end was near. His only comment was: 'I am here as usual, wearing a collar and tie and getting on with the business of managing Celtic.'

The following day the agony was finally over. It happened at 12.20 in the Celtic Suite at Parkhead. Chairman Jack McGinn read out the bleak, prepared statement which was titled, ironically, *Billy McNeill: The End of An Era*. The statement continued: 'The six members of the board decided, without external advice but with the greatest of regret about the manner and nature of excessive media speculation in the past few weeks, that the present era has to end.

'Everyone recognises Billy McNeill has served Celtic faithfully, as player and manager, over a long period, and that he will always be welcome at the club. But the club's supporters have been starved of success for two seasons. They have seen the club spend on new players in the past year. And they expect the board to make a fresh start.'

The reaction from the fans was one of sympathy for McNeill – the man they called Caesar – and anger at the way the board had handled his sacking.

McNeill said later: 'This is my saddest day. In football you have to expect such things may eventually happen to you. Unfortunately, it has happened to me today and now I simply have to get on with my life.'

Terry Cassidy was blamed by many as the real force behind McNeill's departure. But, to this day, he denies the decision had anything to do with him. It was, he claims, a decision made FIVE MONTHS earlier, in January at a secret board meeting. Cassidy said: 'I had only been in the job weeks and before the end of January the Celtic board had one of their secret meetings. They were very good at secret meetings. They held it at the SFA headquarters and I was invited along. The subject was Billy McNeill and they decided that Billy McNeill had to go.

'In the light of what happened it is important to realise what went on at this meeting. They decided that Billy McNeill had to go and they said to me, "What do you think about Billy McNeill?" I said, "I hardly know the man. I've only been here a couple of weeks. I don't know whether he's any good as a manager or not. I've no idea. Ask me again in a month's time when I've had time to assess the situation and then I'll either say 'yes, he's good' or 'no, he's not'."

'Anyway the decision was taken that Billy McNeill should go. What happened then was they said they can't do it now because the cup's coming up and that might upset the fans so we'll have to wait until after the cup game.'

The next time Cassidy recalled talking to the directors about McNeill's possible sacking was on 11 May at the match against St Johnstone in Perth. He said: 'We were in the boardroom at half-time and three of the directors were muttering among themselves. I joined them and they said Billy must go now. We'll give him two more games then he goes.

'So the two games come and Celtic don't do very well and he's still there. Then they say, well, we'd better not do it now because the Rangers game is coming up.

'I asked them if anyone had talked to Billy to say to him they are not satisfied with his performance. Have they said, for example, is there anything we can do to help? And they said no.

'We are into May and the decision they took was in January. We were then coming up to the end of the season and by this time I've a pretty clear idea how bad a state the club's in. It was important we got results on the field to buy time to do all the things which are necessary off the field. So I wanted this thing clarified as well.

'In order to try and bring things to a head I sent the board a memo. The first part was if you decide to keep Billy McNeill you have to give him a contract. That's all I had to say about if they kept him. I then went on to say if you decide to get rid of him this is how you must handle it. I went into great lengths on how they should handle it. How the man is treated with dignity and looked after.

'I believe one of the board members leaked that memo, a confidential memo to directors only. The media then spent a fortnight crucifying me, saying I had written a memo on sacking Billy McNeill.

'I didn't recommend anything. It was a board decision, not mine. The first bit of the memo on retaining Billy McNeill was ignored. The last bit was interpreted as a master plan of mine to sack Billy McNeill.

'The board had found an excuse month after month for not doing it and as chief executive I was sitting there watching this farce being promulgated. I had to do something to move the issue on.'

At the time of the sacking in May 1991 Cassidy was nowhere to be seen when the news was broken. He said it was down to the board to make their views known. Chairman Jack McGinn did not reveal the time they had sat on their decision. Nor did he mention seeking the views of a chief executive who had only been in the job a few weeks about the future of their manager. The only indications he gave regarding the 'Dare we? Will we?' sacking of McNeill was when he said: 'We did not want to jump into this and make a decision of this magnitude. We thought long and hard about it.' He said the media spotlight over the leaked sacking memo had made the decision all the more difficult for the directors. He added: 'All the noise being made has been created by the media. If the truth be known I think all of us felt deep down that a change was necessary. That, if you like, was probably more cut and dried a few days ago. Basically, at the end of the day, we had to make a decision we felt was best for the interests of Celtic Football Club.'

Cassidy was quite happy for his boss to attend to the mass media. After all, he had to do the job most of the time and sometimes it could be a real bind. But, on an issue as big as this, comment should be made. Someone had to lead the way. No sooner had McGinn's words been digested than Cassidy offered his own comments, opening with the line: 'Let's stop living in the past. The attitude we have to take is this. The King is dead . . . long live the King.

'Part of the problem with Celtic is that people have been living in the past. Now the past, and it is a famous history, can be used in two ways. It can be negative or positive. The negative side is a temptation to dwell on past glories, but let's face it, the European Cup was 24 years ago. Of course that achievement is something to treasure but rather than simply looking back fondly upon it we should be using such a success as a role model for the future.'

Cassidy then went on to tell four former players who had been doing public relations work at the club on match days that they were no longer needed. One of them, Lisbon Lion Jimmy Johnstone, stormed out of a meeting with him and later said he would never return to Parkhead so long as Cassidy was at the club. The other three – Tommy Gemmell, Bobby Murdoch and Dixie Deans – were prepared to accept their lost role.

Cassidy, meantime, was back and busy in his own office and one of the main things on his mind was finding the mole who leaked the sacking document in the first place.

Back at the offices of the *Sun*, the editor and staff were ecstatic. The story was one of the best they had run for months and gave them widespread publicity. Cassidy would have given much to find the mole who fed them the document. But despite weeks of snooping about he never did find out. What can now be revealed is the secret memo found its way to the newspaper from the offices of one Michael Kelly. The public-relations man and Celtic director had been making a few notes and alterations to the proposed news release contained in the Cassidy memo. But despite the sensitivity of the document, it had been read by a member of his staff, copied and then relayed on to a freelance journalist. It was one of several disturbing incidents involving the Parkhead board.

By now Brian Dempsey had had enough. The entire episode further fuelled the resentment and anger he felt for the Celtic directors. It was not an easy decision to take but, he concluded, it had to be done. The letter was duly typed and sent off. No more would his cash be used for the good of Celtic. He had cancelled his sponsorship deals with the club, worth in the region of £250,000 a year. Watching Celtic would now be done from the terracing.

In announcing his decision to the *Evening Times* Dempsey said: 'I have decided that I could no longer give my financial support to the club while it is under the present regime. It would be hypocritical of me to do so. I will continue to support the team as I have always done, but I will be standing on the terracing next season.

'The personal treatment meted out to me is no longer acceptable. There has been a campaign of misinformation that I could simply no longer tolerate. However, I am hopeful justice will be done in the end.'

The loss of that cash was a severe blow to Celtic at a time when they were trying to raise capital for a new stadium. The timing wasn't lost on Cassidy. He was in the midst of talks with Superstadia and others over a future home for the club. Celtic finances were already beginning to give rise for concern and losing money was not what he wanted to hear. He decided Dempsey's comments had to be addressed. And addressed they would be – in a big way.

Three weeks later the club's newspaper, the *Celtic View*, contained a three-page article by Cassidy in which Dempsey figured prominently. In it, details of Dempsey's financial contribution to Celtic were laid out, with chief executive Cassidy claiming Dempsey broke his word over a promise to retain his Skybox at Parkhead – no matter the terms or any price increases.

Dempsey reacted quickly and angrily. He challenged the board to disassociate themselves from the article. He said: 'I resent the tone and content of his article. His personal attack on me and others once again focuses attention on this great club for all the wrong reasons.'

Looking back on the row Cassidy said it was nothing personal against Dempsey. He merely wanted the facts to be reported. He added: 'Every newspaper, almost without fail, was saying Celtic were going to lose anything from a quarter of a million to one million pounds because Brian Dempsey was going to withdraw his backing from Celtic Football Club.

'I kept saying to journalists the story wasn't true. We wouldn't be losing this amount of money. So I released the total amount invoiced to Brian Dempsey for the executive boxes, perimeter advertising and programme advertising. That only came to about £90,000 in total. Brian Dempsey had said he would pledge his continued financial support. I had tried to get the facts across to all newspapers. They had selectively decided to ignore it or to produce whatever they felt like producing. I was in the fortunate position of having the club's newspaper, the *Celtic View*, to inform the fans of the facts.'

Cassidy also drove the point home by writing to some journalists and their editors complaining or criticising them. One even threatened to sue Cassidy after the chief executive wrote to his editor stating: 'Would you please reassure your journalist I know he is stupid. He doesn't have to prove it on a daily basis.'

But the row was quickly lost from the headlines with the appointment within days of Liam Brady as Celtic's new manager.

Only 24 hours earlier Cassidy had said the board would not be rushed into finding a successor to Billy McNeill. The board, it appeared, had decided otherwise.

Brady, the 35-year-old Irishman who played in England and Italy, was in confident mood, declaring: 'You can't guarantee success but I see no reason why Celtic cannot be successful in my first year.'

Cassidy too was in confident mood. He beamed: 'No matter what others reckon, it is my belief this club has made tremendous strides in recent months and I think the appointment of Liam is the final piece in the jigsaw.'

It was not to be the case. An entirely new jigsaw was already in the process of being put together by Dempsey.

Chapter Three

Rebel Rousers

Toronto, Canada, early August 1991.

IT HAD been a long flight. Tiresome but comfortable. And, on first impressions, worth it. This great Canadian city on the shores of Lake Ontario looked just as impressive in real life as it did in the brochures. Tall, glass-fronted skyscrapers. Very tall. Which gleamed in the afternoon sun. And dwarfing them all the CN Tower, at over 1,800 feet the tallest free-standing structure in the world.

The downtown Continental Hotel was equally impressive and sat opposite the varsity sports ground where Scotland were due to play a friendly against Canada in nine months time.

It is a city about twice the size of Glasgow and with twice the number of people. But, thought David Low, not a lot of Celtic supporters. There were, however, enough to justify his presence there.

Now, as he finally settled into his hotel, Low's thoughts

turned towards one of those supporters. The man he was there to meet was Jim Doherty, a wealthy yacht broker and a member of one of the three Celtic dynasties – the Grant family. Doherty, 37, was Canadian but a cousin of Celtic stadium manager and director Tom Grant. It was Doherty who controlled the shares of the Grant family in Canada and who wielded influence over the family shareholders in Northern Ireland. He held about four per cent of the total Celtic shares with family members accounting for another ten per cent.

Low, a 33-year-old financial consultant with an interest in football, was working for Brian Dempsey. His remit was to try and muster enough votes to force changes in the Celtic board should there be enough rebel shareholders to achieve that aim.

Doherty had been very much a long-distance supporter for years. But an upturn in business and the commission on sales of $500,000 yachts had provided him with a comfortable lifestyle and he was now able to travel to Glasgow frequently for matches at Parkhead. His first visit had been five months ago when the tears welled in his eyes as he walked into the stand, savoured an atmosphere he only ever heard about and watched his team beat Old Firm rivals Rangers 3–0 in the league.

On that occasion he met Dempsey and the concerns of the rebel shareholders were expressed to him. Now he was anxious to become actively involved in saving the club he had waited so long to become a real part of.

Low was sipping a cool drink in the cocktail lounge when Doherty arrived. 'We spoke about the club and what we could do to try and get others on our side,' he said. 'I had already met Chris White and Jack McGinn in Glasgow and I remember walking away from the meeting shaking my head. These people had no idea how to run a football club. Not that I did, but as an outsider looking in I could see big trouble with that club.

'David Low and I talked about the problems. Chris White had a tendency to keep everyone in the dark. We had no idea how the club was doing. The demise, the rot, was a little more serious than some of us had imagined. However, we knew it was heading in that direction. At the time we said we needed people with management skills and business acumen to take the club into the next century. I believed Brian Dempsey was one such man and I was devastated when I heard he had been ousted as a director. David and I decided to do a bit of globe-trotting and we set off to gather support from other shareholders.'

The trips included visits to family members in Canada, Northern Ireland and Scotland. In Canada there were four other family members who were shareholders plus five others who were shareholders of Celtic but with no family ties. Four trips were made to County Antrim in Northern Ireland where five of the Grant cousins lived. Visits were paid to ten other shareholders around the Belfast area.

In Scotland there was stadium manager, director and cousin Tom Grant. 'We always got on well,' said Doherty. 'We had our differences but in all fairness to Tom he made some decisions which were right to him at the time but which, we believed, were wrong for the club. However, we knew then the board of directors didn't have control and had to rely on some of the people we were then talking to.'

For David Low it was a change of direction. The following year the now Glasgow-based financial consultant was living in Edinburgh but had followed the Celtic issue with interest. He was regarded by some as something of a football groupie, having been involved with other clubs before, including Hibs who are based in the capital. He was hoping not much about his own background would come out in this campaign. Everyone, it is said, has a skeleton in their cupboard and Low was no different. Only a year ago he had backed the sacking of Dempsey as a director and congratulated Michael Kelly and Chris White for their 'foresight and the efficient manner in which they sought to preserve all that Celtic Football Club stands for'. Now it was a source of embarrassment to him. He remembered at the time Michael Kelly had told him things and lots of shareholders had voted against Dempsey because of what was said. Now, he thought, a lot of the shareholders who supported Kelly and loathed Dempsey were on his side. Fortunately Dempsey did not hold grudges.

Back in Glasgow, Dempsey was relatively happy with the progress being made. Proxy votes were building up. Slowly but surely. And the campaign was building momentum. The first main breakaway group of fans had emerged. And they were increasing in numbers. The Independent Celtic Supporters' Association – later to emerge as the Affiliation of Registered Celtic Supporters' Clubs – were planning a meeting to discuss the future of the club. They set a date three months away and invited the Celtic board to be represented.

Just over a month later Chairman Jack McGinn stepped down with Kevin Kelly taking his place. The pressure was beginning to tell. McGinn said the reason was his commitments to the game's governing body, the Scottish Football Association, as treasurer. About suggestions there might be other reasons he said: 'I can do nothing about speculation.'

At the time McGinn was not given much option about the timing of his resignation as Chairman. To sweeten the move he was made the offer of a financial package to compensate the loss of his Chairman's allowance and to allow him to continue with his SFA activities. The financial part of that deal was never honoured.

During the run-up to the end of the year, the hoped for improvement in the team's performance was not materialising. Celtic won five of their league matches, lost five and drew four. The mood of the rebel supporters was not good when the day of the meeting came on 1 December.

Terry Cassidy was the solitary representative from Celtic. He calmly took his seat on stage at Shettleston Town Hall and faced an angry barrage of questions from the 400-strong audience. 'Yes.' Celtic would have one of the best stadiums in Europe by 1994. 'No.' He couldn't say exactly where the cash would come from. 'Yes.' It would be difficult to achieve. 'No.' He couldn't say exactly where the cash would come from. 'Yes.' It would be difficult to achieve. 'No.' The board is not split.

The fans left the meeting unconvinced. Among them long-time Celtic board critic Professor Tom Carbery, a former lecturer at Strathclyde Business School. At the meeting he blasted: 'Where is the money? It is just not going to happen. I am in my late sixties and I don't think I will ever see, in my lifetime, Celtic with a stadium comparable to Rangers.'

But the next day new Chairman Kevin Kelly backed his beleaguered chief executive. He said: 'We will have a great stadium and I am confident we will find the money to achieve that. Terry Cassidy is right to say the board is more united than ever and we are looking forward to the future.'

Cassidy then came out with guns blazing again firing shot after shot at his critics and the club's Old Firm rivals Rangers. He revealed he was fed up having the success of Rangers constantly thrown in his face. The chief executive said: 'If somebody from Rangers says something it is believed. If somebody from Celtic says something it is not believed. I happen to believe that Rangers have bigger problems.

'I don't care about Rangers. I don't think about Rangers. I don't, like a lot of people, have an obsession about Rangers.

'People at Parkhead are working their little socks off trying to get things right. No credit is given to anybody at

Celtic. We are working for the future of Celtic and we will get results.'

Jim Doherty read the words contained in a newspaper report which had been sent to him. A wry smile spread below his thick moustache. Oh really? thought Doherty, we'll see about that.

The Celtic directors rattled through their annual general meeting in December without much fuss. Yes, debts were growing, but they could handle that, they claimed. What they couldn't handle – or claim to – were the results on the field. Celtic crashed 3–1 at home to Rangers on New Year's Day and followed that three days later with a 2–1 home defeat, this time by Hearts, which left Brady's men 13 points off the pace in the league with still four months of the season to go,

Just over a week later Cassidy and Brady were at loggerheads. The chief executive said skipper Paul McStay had until the end of the month to sign a new contract. A fuming Brady countered: 'There's no deadline. We haven't put an offer in front of Paul yet.'

The incident seemed to have been sparked off by the pressures on and off the field over the past few weeks. But both men knew it was deeper than that. It went all the way back to the summer tour in Dublin in July 1991. Cassidy recalled: 'Liam had only been in the job a few weeks when they went off for a pre-season tour in Ireland. My wife had not long died after her illness and I decided to go out and join the team.

'I knew some people in Dublin and had met them for a few drinks then I went back to the hotel. The assistant manager Tommy Craig was sitting with physio Brian Scott and a couple of journalists. I thought I would have a drink with them and sat down. I said something like "defenders are ten a penny, they're easy to find. The key is really good forwards." The journalists then said something and I suppose I had insulted the journalists.

41

'I hadn't seen Liam Brady at all that night. The next morning I came down to breakfast and sat next to Liam and director Jack McGinn. I got the big cold treatment. Brady wouldn't even speak to me and I didn't know why. I had no idea. All through that trip Brady barely said a thing to me and made it quite clear he didn't want anything to do with me. I let the whole thing ride because the guy was new to the job and was settling in and the whole thing was new to him.

'After the tour a piece appeared in the newspapers saying Brady was going to demand that I go and that there had been a meeting in Jack McGinn's bedroom in Ireland where Brady had said it was him or me. I called Brady into my office back at Parkhead and told him that whatever was upsetting him it was second-hand because it hadn't happened between him and me. I told him I could only trace it back to that night in Dublin and that at least one of those present had gone back to him and given him a distorted version of what I'd said. I told him that if he was going to be in management he had to learn to be objective and not to be childish and not to be silly. So if there was something bothering him he should tell me. He said there was no problem.

'What happened next was at a board meeting. Liam spoke about the way he saw the future and the playing needs. And then all of a sudden said, "And I demand the chief executive is fired" and "I couldn't possibly work with him". I just sat there and asked why. Michael Kelly spoke up and told him it was not his job to recommend who is or is not chief executive of Celtic Football Club and there was no way I was going to be removed. He told Brady that was the matter closed.

'I kept trying to talk to Liam Brady. I kept saying to him that he didn't know what sort of a board he was dealing with. I said he was very young in management, didn't know a lot about management, and told him one of my jobs was to help him. Then I said if he wanted to get things through the board and wanted new players then I would be supportive of him.'

The relationship between Cassidy and Brady did not improve after that. However, the row was overshadowed with the rumours then spreading about the moves by Doherty and Low four months earlier to obtain proxy votes. While all eyes were on Celtic, Doherty and Low, with the quiet assistance of Dempsey, had increased the voting power of the rebels to close on 40 per cent. Emerging with them was the financial clout offered by Dempsey's allies – his business partner John Keane and millionaire exile Eddie Keane. Eddie is a former carpet warehouse owner but no relation to John. He had sold up and settled for the good life in Bermuda.

If the rebels could swing Doherty's cousin, director Tom Grant, and Chairman Kevin Kelly, they would have control.

Suddenly the scenario was frighteningly brought home to Chris White and Michael Kelly, who were the two who effectively controlled the club. The other two directors, Jack McGinn and Jimmy Farrell, had always shown support for Dempsey but their shareholding was not substantial. They were, therefore, considered only minor players in the board game.

The board had been trying to give the impression they were united but it appeared they were far from it. All they need, pondered Doherty as he read the latest cuttings to reach him in Toronto, is a gentle push and the entire dynasty rule begins to crumble. Now was the time for a few timely and well-chosen words: 'Shareholders and supporters here in Canada and elsewhere are concerned at what is going on at Celtic. It seems to me, even though I am a long way from what is happening, that some of the directors are putting personal interests first. I'd like to see that stopped.'

Doherty then took an even higher profile, arriving in Glasgow and appearing on Scottish Television to outline his takeover plans.

Doherty's broadside hit the board of directors at Parkhead with full force. He won a meeting with Chairman Kevin Kelly but not before Cassidy returned the broadside. The chief executive was back in full swing soaking up the flak aimed at the directors and firing back. He described Doherty and his crew as 'a joke' and dismissed reports that Chris White and Michael Kelly could be on their way out of Celtic Park. In an interview with the *Evening Times* Cassidy said: 'I don't feel threatened and I don't believe the board do either. These people who talk about taking over Celtic are a joke. I am fed up with people trying to dig Celtic's grave and bury them. The sooner we get this out of the way the sooner we can get on with the job of running Celtic.'

But it was obvious certain board members did indeed feel threatened. The following day Doherty and Low met Kevin Kelly in Tom Grant's house. They said they wanted to become directors in place of White and Michael Kelly.

Grant was now supportive of his cousin and his attempts backed by Low and Dempsey. Kevin Kelly though was as unsure as he normally was. Doherty concluded that they might have to call an emergency general meeting to force changes.

The board were beginning to get the message that secretive shareholdings which lie in the hands of a small group of individuals were out of tune with the modern game. And the other shareholders – with plenty of voice from ordinary fans – were making sure White, Kelly and company were hearing loud and clear. But all the talk now was about whether the rebels could pull in enough shareholders to win the day. Already there were reports of Celtic's 20,000 shares soaring from their normally static and board dictated price of £3 to £165. It was said that was the price being paid by Doherty, Low and Dempsey to secure the votes. The truth was the amount changing hands was substantially more than that. A figure of £250 had already been paid out.

On paper the rebels couldn't buy the shares outright because any transactions had to be approved by the Celtic board and they were unlikely to do that. So legal deals were done whereby the proxy votes were obtained with the rights to the shares going to the purchaser if and when they could be transferred. Financial experts still regarded it as the first time there had been open dealing in Celtic shares.

More intrigue rose to the surface with claims and counter-claims as to who held the key votes and which way they could go. Director Jack McGinn's shareholding was small but by going with the rebels he would not only give them valuable support but maybe convince a few others to join him.

But within days there was a new story for the media which stopped everyone dead in their tracks as the board announced an astonishing twist. Michael Kelly and Chris White decided the introduction of a fresh financial face could save their bacon. And at the scheduled board meeting on 21 February a seventh director was added to the board. The fact that he got his seat on the casting vote of Chairman Kevin Kelly showed on whose side he lined up with.

The new man was one David Smith – a Scot, a big name in City of London financial circles, an old friend of Chris White and the first Protestant to sit on the Celtic board. Kevin Kelly announced: 'We are delighted to have been able to attract to the board someone of David Smith's calibre, experience, contacts and ability. It is, in my estimation, the boldest and most imaginative appointment ever made to a Celtic board. It enables the board to face the real issues confronting the club, and to demonstrate to shareholders that their interests are being addressed in a professional and positive manner.'

The board had earlier considered, but rejected, a proposal that the dissident shareholder group led by Doherty and Low be given two seats on the board. That proposal was backed by Grant, McGinn and Farrell. Their rebellious move was regarded as treason by Michael Kelly and Chris White. The following week White and the Kellys acted swiftly to crush those who dared oppose them. They called the extraordinary general meeting the rebels were contemplating – but with the purpose of removing the dissidents Grant and Farrell.

The skirmishes had led to a full-blown battle which promised to be bloody and brutal. The Whites and the Kellys believed they had done enough to show they had control. But while they sat back and waited for what they saw as a sure victory, the rebels were busy. Dempsey had called his group to arms and they sat around the table to draw up their battle plan. The ousted director knew that now was the time to put words into action. He sat at the head of the table in his office boardroom. He was listening as Low and Doherty argued the best tactics but his mind was wandering. The killer words spoken to him by Michael Kelly on the night he was ousted came back to haunt him as they had often before. 'This is something we must do.' But Dempsey knew it was his turn to utter the words and turn them against the men who humiliated him.

This, he thought, is something WE must do.

Chapter Four

First Blood

Three days before the EGM. Glasgow, Friday,
27 March 1992.

NO-ONE paid any attention to the small, bespectacled man
as he got out of the car. He was smart in appearance apart
from one curious piece of dress – a brown checked cap
pulled over his head. It looked totally out of place against the
expensive camel hair coat atop an equally expensive suit.

He climbed the few steps into the reception area of the
offices of accountants Pannell Kerr Forster overlooking the
River Clyde on the south side of the city centre. After
exchanging greetings he was led into the plush meeting
room with dark leather seats neatly arranged around the
black, highly polished mahogany table. A small posse of
advisers followed him inside.

Unassuming and thinly built, his appearance was
deceiving – as many who had crossed Fergus McCann had
already discovered to their cost. There was a hint of Scots
in his Canadian accent as he spoke: 'Gentlemen, have the
press releases been prepared?'

Across the river and a few miles west Brian Dempsey, David Low and Jim Doherty were still making calls and deals to try and build on their growing support of shareholders. Dempsey knew McCann. He knew him during his short spell on the board when McCann had offered a £6.5 million low-interest loan to the club which was rejected. He knew he was back in town and had spoken to him a few days previously. He also knew the Montreal-based self-made millionaire wanted to see the downfall of the present Celtic board.

Equally, he knew he couldn't deal with him. Not at this stage. The two did not see eye-to-eye on the way change should be brought about and on how the future of the great club should be shaped.

Dempsey had found another couple of shareholders willing to sell. The total shares were minimal but every vote counted at this stage. Low had discovered that the board needed 51 per cent of the votes to oust the other two directors and have their way. But the rebels were almost neck and neck with the board, having won over many of the doubtful voters to their camp.

The weekend was almost on them. It was going to be close and they all knew that. Dempsey, though, still had an ace up his sleeve. He dispatched Low to Edinburgh to deal it.

Back along the river the media had now descended on the offices of Pannell Kerr Forster. Lights were switched on, cameras set up and microphones placed on the table. Seated reporters crowded on one side of the room and photographers crouched over them. Enter, stage right, 50-year-old Fergus McCann. The man who was about to offer to save Celtic.

The former accountant who quit Scotland in 1964 had never forgotten his roots. He was raised in the mining town of Kilsyth and had been social convenor of the local Croy Celtic Supporters' Club. In Canada he made his millions sending Americans to play on Scotland's golf courses through a sports promotions firm he had built from nothing and which he had sold for a reported £15 million. Now he divided his time between homes in Montreal, Arizona and Bermuda.

The newsmen and sports writers listened intently as he outlined his plan. A new McCann company called Celtic's Future plc would raise £17.28 million which would be offered for investment in Celtic. It would include £7.2 million of his own cash, £5 million from Scottish and overseas investors and £5 million from the fans through new shares.

'This is not a hostile manoeuvre,' he said. 'It is intended to be a positive one. I have the resources financially to get this plan moving forward.'

A new stadium at a new site was not, though, among his plans. He wanted a three-phase redevelopment at Parkhead. 'It is important that this work begins as soon as possible otherwise the future of Celtic as a major club is in jeopardy.'

Through his plan the directors would not be bought out. 'There would be a new share issue and current shareholders would benefit from that. They would become a smaller number of a larger shareholding.' He would be seeking 50 per cent of the shares and would devote all his attention to Celtic. But he would not proceed without the backing of the fans. He said: 'If I don't get that I won't go ahead. It is not my intention to do anything against the will of the supporters or the shareholders.'

McCann stressed he was not involved with the rebel shareholders led by Doherty and Dempsey. But he added: 'I commend their efforts to consolidate a group of shareholder supporters who want to see the club refinanced, rebuilt and reorganised. I have announced my plans today because I want to make it clear it is an independent offer not connected with any rebel group and I will not be at Monday's EGM.'

So McCann had laid his cards on the table and staked his claim.

It was, thought Dempsey, a bit of a gamble but the odds were not that bad. McCann was hedging his bets a bit. Dempsey had yet to contact the Celtic board with his offer. Now he was ready to do so – after Monday when the result of the power struggle would be known.

Quite shrewd. Very clever.

It was getting late. The telephone buzzed. It was Low and things were looking good. Dempsey allowed himself a smile.

While McCann was busy outlining his plans, Celtic's longest-serving director Jimmy Farrell, 70, was appealing to shareholders to exercise their votes carefully. Farrell was making a last-ditch effort to hold on to his seat and influence the floating voters. In a letter to all shareholders he warned against moving up to a new stadium site and criticised the way in which David Smith was brought on to the board. On a move to a new stadium site – with Cambuslang emerging favourite – he said: 'It is hazardous both in financial terms and is bedevilled with technical and planning difficulties. This concern I have voiced to the board. It is not too drastic to argue that should this plan be adopted it could result in the possible liquidation of Celtic.' On Smith he asked: 'What facts did he not tell you?'

Celtic Chairman Kevin Kelly took the cue to get in on the act. Of McCann's offer he said: 'The conditions attaching to his proposals and the absence of firm underwriting meant they could not be pursued by the board.' The chairman, like Farrell, also wrote to share-holders. In his letter he said: 'I, like most other Celtic people, was disturbed by the increasingly strident press comment. There was no apparent reason for this within the club and it became obvious that the campaign was inspired by a disparate group outside the club who had made no formal approach to the board.

'These reports unequivocally linked Mr Farrell and Mr Grant with that disparate group and, by implication, with their stated intentions.

'In order to clarify their position Mr Farrell and Mr Grant were invited by other directors to dissociate themselves from the statements of those outside parties. This they declined to do.'

It was obvious both sides were sweating a bit over what was to be a long weekend. The tension was building. The confrontation was getting closer.

On the field the team were having a great run. The previous week they had beaten Rangers 2–0 at Ibrox. Now they were celebrating a 3–1 victory over Dundee United at Celtic Park which stretched their run of victories to nine in a row.

All of the directors were at the park for the game. So too were the rebels. In 48 hours they would return to line up against each other.

The public confrontation had all the elements Celtic fans could wish for: fast and furious action. Tackling from all sides. Goals scored for and against – including own goals. And big spending on the transfer market, even if it was on shares.

Frantic telephone calls were made over Sunday as Dempsey, Doherty and Low tried to sway those shareholders still regarded as 'undecided'. Sunday was a good day to get people at home and some deals were made. The balance was shifting – but not quite enough.

Then the long-awaited Monday morning arrived. Dempsey was up at dawn – about an hour before his usual rise. He couldn't sleep. There was too much on his mind. He showered and dressed and set off on the normal 20-minute drive to his office.

The EGM would kick off at noon but moves were still afoot. Dempsey pulled up outside his office after a quicker drive due to the lack of traffic at that earlier time of the morning. The roads started to get busier as traffic heaved into the city. Shops and offices opened up and staff began to arrive at Celtic Park.

The time, thought Dempsey, is about now. All over west central Scotland sheriff officers set out calling at the homes of 16 Celtic shareholders. Dempsey and his group had struck. They had applied for and won a court order banning 16 shareholders from voting at the crucial EGM. At the Court of Session in Edinburgh Lord Mayfield had granted an interim interdict to Dempsey who alleged the 16 named people were not entitled to vote. Dempsey claimed the shares were registered unlawfully in their names. The interdict meant the 16 could not use the votes attached to their shares. It also stopped them granting a proxy vote to anyone else. What Low had uncovered in the Register of Companies in Edinburgh was that shares had been transferred illegally.

The move stunned White and the Kellys. Their confidence had disappeared in one sudden swoop. They were, however, still claiming they had enough support for victory. A defiant Michael Kelly said: 'The interdict does not affect all of the shares held by the 16 shareholders. The original proposals will be voted on.' He maintained that Farrell and Grant would go and Smith would be voted on to the board.

But what was supposed to be a show of strength by the three directors was now a struggle for survival. Frantic behind-the-scenes moves were launched by Celtic as the board consulted their lawyers and as the EGM drew even closer.

It was all smiles from Dempsey, Doherty and Low as they arrived at Parkhead for the crunch confrontation. The two pm meeting was delayed half an hour as the threatened three sought a way out. But there was nothing they could do.

There was an air of expectancy at Celtic Park as

shareholders packed into the boardroom for the EGM. The Kellys and White trooped in with the other directors. First of the three proposals was the re-appointment of Jimmy Farrell. Each proposal would be voted on firstly by a show of hands. If it did not go the way the Kellys and White wanted they would then call for a poll where those shareholders with the most shares would have the greater say. The show of hands went the way of the rebels with victory for Farrell. The trio then called for a poll.

Half an hour passed as the share vote was counted. It was a tense time for the rebels and Farrell – and for the trio trying to remove him. With the effect of the interdict both sides were close on the voting shares they could call on. The undecided shareholders, the 'floaters', now held the balance of power.

Then came the result. It was close, but Farrell had won. His 27-year association with the board would continue.

Next came the re-appointment of Grant. Again this was won by the rebels on a show of hands. But this time the trio did not demand a poll. Dempsey and Doherty looked at each other. Something was wrong. I'll bet, thought Dempsey, a deal has been done here.

He was right. When the third proposal for the appointment of David Smith came, Grant voted for him. It wasn't enough for the show of hands to reject the motion but with Grant now obviously on the opposition side it would go through in the poll. It did and Smith became the seventh director.

That annoyed Dempsey and his group as they had effectively saved Grant's bacon only for him to turn and support the trio. But it was still a night of victory for the rebels with the board having suffered their biggest defeat ever.

Michael Kelly looked grim-faced as he and his fellow directors appeared in front of the assembled media to announce the results of what had been a marathon eight-hour meeting. He said the directors now had an 'agreement' and were united again. He added: 'The in-fighting we have seen over the past few months we will not see again. The fact we are now talking about stability suggests all the pain was worthwhile.'

But Doherty would not be conned. The Canadian said: 'We are not finished yet. The shareholders have let the board know we are not going to sit back and take any more. We want this club pulled back together and we are still talking to our lawyers.'

Grant also put on a brave face and denied he had done a deal. He said: 'I voted for Jimmy Farrell and he voted for me. My vote for David Smith was in the interests of the club. It is simply not true that I jumped sides. What we have done is try to convince the Kellys and the Whites that the others will not go away. They cannot continue with the attitude that it is my ball and you will play my game. I just wish we had managed to put our pride behind us and sorted this out without all of this.'

Farrell looked to be the only director with a grin on his face. He urged his boardroom rivals not to close the door on Dempsey. 'As far as Brian Dempsey is concerned, one should have an open mind,' he said.

Doherty, Low and Grant headed off together from Parkhead for a few drinks. Dempsey headed home. It had been another long day but a very satisfying one – and important. Looking back on the night he recalled the significance of that meeting. He said: 'That EGM was arguably the most significant watershed in Celtic's history. For 105 years things had all been done within the boardroom but now, for once, they went out publicly to try and remove two directors we knew we could not be beaten. They needed a 51 per cent majority to do that and we had successfully blocked the extra votes they needed.

'I must admit that I was apprehensive that day and scared to count my chickens but we won it well and no matter what the Kellys and Whites tried to do from then on, they knew they could be stopped. Stopping them that night was the most critical aspect of the entire campaign because they now had no choice but to recognise that the force against them was a formidable adversary. So they found themselves in great difficulty in having lost that night and having to make a deal with Tom Grant. It was a very significant night.'

Significant also was the appointment of Smith as a director. The 47-year-old accountant was seen as the answer to Celtic's dwindling income and growing overdraft. But there was one man unhappy with that appointment as well as other events. He was adamant the personality clashes thrown up at the EGM would not overshadow the issue. Terry Cassidy thought he was the one who had been brought in to do the commercial job. There was, however, no mention of how the appointment would affect Cassidy who now faced a clash of jobs with Smith.

Cassidy was quick to react though and marked out his territory quite clearly. He sent a memo to staff telling them Smith was a non-executive director and 'if he asks for anything clear it with me first'.

Cassidy began to climb to an even higher profile at Celtic Park and made some of his most sweeping statements yet. If he had ever thought twice about giving an interview he most certainly wouldn't now. His first aim was clear enough. He wanted a seat on the board – just like the one David Smith had. Oh, and he also wanted Parkhead bulldozed.

According to Cassidy there were only two options facing the directors over the stadium plans. Build a new one for £70 million or stay at Celtic Park, which would of course be demolished, and build a new version for £45 million.

Cassidy was in confident mood as he outlined his thoughts. 'There have been some very positive developments. People don't understand what we are saying. Celtic will not have to fund the entire project. We are talking about building a stadium in partnership with someone else, which means Celtic may own 100 per cent of it or nothing at all.

'If we choose to build on another site, Celtic will play at Parkhead until the new stadium is ready. If we stay at Parkhead, we would build a new stadium from scratch with a playing surface over what is now the car park. If the masterplan doesn't come about, we have a very good scheme to fall back on.'

He then chose his words carefully. David Smith was the man now promising the cash for all of this, thought Cassidy, so let's give him his place. 'David Smith has a proven track record and financial connections which will help us find additional money for the stadium.'

That, he thought, will do. For now.

He even thought the board was 'more united now than ever' despite the newspapers being full of reports that the knives were now out for Michael Kelly.

But public relations man Kelly seemed as confident as Cassidy and it appeared he had every right to be so. Before the dust had time to settle Kelly and White had been to the club's solicitors to have a document drawn up and a new company formed. The existence of some kind of 'agreement' was mentioned at the EGM but was passed over in the turmoil of the night. This was to be their protection for the next ten years . . . or so they thought.

Chapter Five

The Dreamers

Sunday, 5 April 1992, 9 am.

IT had been a tiring week. The telephone had gone non-stop. Now at last a rest. Probably, thought Dempsey, it's the same for everyone else who has been involved in this battle. Michael Kelly is likely to be wandering about in his dressing gown. Tom Grant will probably be tucked up in the safety of his bed. Kevin Kelly in the kitchen making breakfast. Chris White in the room with the drawn curtains. And, mused Dempsey, David Smith glad he was back at his home in London.

He scanned the Sunday newspapers. There was still a lot being reported about the EGM. Repercussions, innuendo and speculation. There were also articles about Dempsey: 'The Man who is making Celtic his Business' and 'What motivates Parkhead Pretender Brian Dempsey'. Interesting but not particularly informing.

What motivated Dempsey right now was the desire to rise, venture forth into the sunshine and watch his son play rugby. Strange that, he thought, a father so heavily into football and his son plays rugby. Still, that's the sport favoured by his school. And anyway, it's good to get away from football for a day. A nice relaxing day then back to business tomorrow. Business without Celtic for a while.

How wrong he was. Michael Kelly was, by now, well into the Sunday newspapers and wasn't at all happy with comments Dempsey had been making. It appeared there were rumours that Dempsey, the scourge of the Celtic board, planned to return in an even more threatening manner. Kelly and Co didn't like that idea one little bit. Especially when Dempsey had denied the rumours by saying: 'I told Kelly to his face that I didn't admire or respect what he was doing at Celtic.'

The next day Michael Kelly was back in the headlines hitting out at Dempsey. The *Evening Times* – under the headline 'Celtic's new war of words' – carried an article which read: 'Celtic director Michael Kelly today accused Brian Dempsey of "getting personal". Kelly is unhappy over remarks made by axed director Dempsey which stated he would "not sit round the same table as Michael Kelly". And today Kelly hit back . . .'

The article went on to quote Kelly as saying: 'I am disappointed about Brian's remarks. When I spoke to him after the club's EGM last week our conversation was absolutely cordial. Now it all seems to have degenerated into an issue about personalities.'

Exactly, thought Dempsey, what Mr Kelly is getting embroiled in right now.

Dempsey left the issue alone. He had vowed to allow the club time to breathe and let the directors prove they could indeed do a job at Celtic. That was fine because Kelly and White had more important things on their minds. The 'agreement' they had referred to at the EGM was taking shape. As far as they were concerned they would soon have no need to worry much about Mr Dempsey. Anyway, they were well on their way to the 'big announcement' which would prove them right, deflect any attention away from the rebels and have all Celtic fans jumping with glee. The expensive consultants at London-based Superstadia had at last come up with a preferred stadium plan and had convinced the board it would work.

Just over a week later the Celtic Suite at Parkhead was prepared for the big day. Seats were arranged for the media, speeches were photocopied, refreshments arranged and drawings paraded on display boards.

The next morning the journalists and photographers duly streamed into Celtic Park for the 'big announcement'. There was a hush as the lights dimmed a little. The words appeared from an overhead projector: 'Celtic supporters have had a dream. That dream could be in our grasp at Cambuslang . . .' Celtic's new £100 million home was unveiled.

Chairman Kevin Kelly smiled for the first time in weeks and told the assembled Press: 'This is the most exciting day in the history of Celtic Football Club.'

Members of the media looked at each other. If this was really going to happen then they were witnessing a small piece of footballing history. They now had in their hands a news release issued by director Michael Kelly's public relations firm – the same firm receiving thousands of pounds each year from Celtic Football Club.

One man was named as a contact for the media on that news release – a man who appeared to wallow in the role and who later asked that his name was not mentioned in connection with Celtic stories – Mike Stanger. The former BBC press spokesman later found himself under severe pressure. But, for the moment, he was the spokesman for the spokesman who spoke for Celtic.

The news release contained enough facts. In fact it contained a lot of facts. Too many facts, in fact, for too many people to take in. It was also badly written, from a journalistic point of view. The release began: 'Celtic Football Club today submitted an application for outline planning permission for a major new stadium complex to be built on a 30-hectare site at Cambuslang.'

The question came from a reporter near the back of the assembled audience: 'Sorry, what?' It fell on deaf ears.

'The application was submitted to Glasgow District Council, following positive meetings with the Glasgow Development Agency over the use of the land. The GDA have given their backing to the scheme and are doing what they can to facilitate it.'

The questions began, but were quickly lost: 'Sorry, what?'

'The scheme proposed is a careful blend of sporting and commercial developments, each designed to complement the other in terms of the facilities provided and the mutually-supportive funding.'

'Sorry, what?'

There then appeared 15 one-line statements highlighting the benefits of the new 'dream'.

'Sorry, what?'

While journalists sat and tried to digest the first wave of public relations, the second wave struck. The finance. How much it would cost for each phase and where the money was supposed to come from.

'Capital allowances, sponsorship, box sales, preferential seating bonds, development land sales, the Football Trust, and other public sector associated commercial developments, sustained by increased income generation.'

'Sorry, what?'

Never in the field of Celtic human endeavour had so much been offered to so many by so few. The completion date for this grand project was the 'second half of 1994'.

Kevin Kelly was now in full flow and the immortal lines were repeated: 'Celtic supporters have had a dream. That dream could be in our grasp at Cambuslang, which is so close to our traditional heartland. But we need to pull it together and make it happen. Our task is to make sure that all genuine Celtic supporters have a chance to participate in the development in a meaningful and uplifting manner.'

'Sorry, what?'

'For far too long, the Celtic board have faced a non-stop barrage of ill-considered criticism from uninformed people of dubious motivation. Now, it is possible for Celtic's true supporters to see that constructive and imaginative progress has all the while been made behind the scenes towards achieving what we all want to see – the very best for the most faithful fans in the world.'

'Sorry, what?'

But the media didn't have to wait long. Michael Kelly's Michael Stanger also produced a three-page background report to 'aid' journalists. Then, in stepped new director David Smith to announce that Celtic would, if the preferred course is followed, only be tenants, thus ensuring a place for the club to play 'into perpetuity'.

'Sorry, is that another name for timeshare?'

But all was later to be revealed in the club's newspaper. Celtic would have a 52,000 all-seater stadium with a 'space-age' roof, two railway stations, a 200-bed hotel, a Celtic heritage museum, cinemas and shops. The centrepiece stadium would include mobile acoustic curtains so that it could be turned into a 15,000-seat pop concert arena.

Chairman Kelly added: 'All the homework has been done, with months spent on researching the scheme itself and possible ways of funding it. The supporters will be told of developments as soon as possible but I believe the fact they now see Celtic Football Club are involved in a scheme of this sort is reward in itself.

'I feel the same sense of history the founding fathers of this club must have felt more than 100 years ago. When they first stood on their chosen site at Parkhead they saw only derelict land, a mine shaft and a graveyard. I've been looking round the land at Cambuslang trying to imagine where the first goal will be scored.'

Probably an own goal, thought Dempsey later.

Everyone, though, loved the idea as it was unveiled to them. The board did. The players did. The fans did. Dempsey did – for different reasons. Even Terry Cassidy did. His words were probably the most meaningful at the time. He said: 'This is the start of the most exciting era in this club's great history. But it is only the first step on a long and difficult road to our destination. It is a hugely significant step and is based upon achieving a stadium which will be the best we could possibly hope to have.'

There were, however, two notable absentees. Directors Jimmy Farrell and Jack McGinn.

Farrell was already on record as saying a move to Cambuslang could bankrupt the club and they didn't want that repeated. McGinn had already handed over the chairmanship and his views were also not required. Anyway, they were not part of the new 'agreement' which was nearing conclusion in the form of a written document.

What a surprise, thought Dempsey. What a really big surprise. Here we have Superstadia with their great plans and drawings and telling everyone what a marvellous stadium Celtic are going to have. I wonder, he asked, just how much they were getting in fees for this exercise?

Dempsey was already aware Michael Kelly was acting as public relations consultant to Superstadia as well as Celtic. He didn't like that and the possible conflict of interest it represented. Dempsey recalled the first time he had met with Superstadia. 'It was while I was a director at Celtic,' he said. 'I met the people from the organisation with Jack McGinn. I dismissed them then. I told Jack and the Superstadia people themselves that they wouldn't be able to do anything for us. They obviously came back on the scene in a big way.'

The timing of the Cambuslang announcement was another situation Dempsey remembers for reasons of his own. He said: 'It happened two weeks after the EGM and was, in my opinion, a panic measure by the board of directors. They were under pressure from all sides to come up with the goods to prove they were united when, in fact, we knew they were not.

'But we had to give them the chance. We had said we would. Now they had come out with Cambuslang. Ironically it was to be that announcement which effectively led to their downfall.'

At the time, though, Dempsey, Doherty and Low were not to know that the announcement then would provide them with plenty of ammunition for the future. 'The priority at that stage was to keep buying up shares,' said Dempsey. 'After the EGM a lot of shareholders had come to us and said they had realised that there was no way forward now. The club was locked in a conflict which would go to the death for one side or the other and the best they could do was get their money and get out, so we kept buying.

'We had to strike whatever deal we could. Some shares were bought for £150 or £175 and others for as much as £250 and that was at a time when the directors were exchanging or transferring shares for around £3. It was a bit of a gamble but it was one we had to take at the time.

'We were marking time. What started to happen then was lack of success on the field, disgruntlement among the fans and the manager clearly unhappy with what was going on around him. The chief executive was clearly at loggerheads with everyone and the media were becoming embroiled in all sorts of situations through the chief executive. Then came the irony with the Chairman publicly remonstrating and rebutting the chief executive for having misled the press by saying planning consent for Cambuslang would be coming in a couple of weeks.

Things were not looking good at that early stage for the board.'

The rebels would not go away and the board knew it.

Michael Kelly, Chris White and David Smith looked for directions. But it seemed the mist had closed over their eyes. They weren't getting very far or very fast with Cambuslang. Money was the main reason.

It was at that stage their thoughts turned again to the little man from Canada. The McCann guy who had disappeared after the EGM back to Montreal. It was then the plot was hatched.

The five directors – who had already read a draft of their 'agreement' – met. After the meeting it was decided Michael Kelly and David Smith would head out to Canada for a nice trip and a chat with Fergus McCann.

McCann was back in his plush Montreal apartment when he got the call. He agreed to see the two directors. But McCann was suspicious of them. He had been suspicious of most Celtic directors he had met. They had not appeared to be too keen on his offer just before the EGM, so what did they want now?

The last time he had offered money was two years ago when he had proposed a low-interest loan to revamp the seating at Parkhead. He hadn't asked for any involvement or equity. He had flown to Glasgow for a meeting and was kept waiting several days before Jack McGinn agreed to see him. A large proportion of the £6.5 million he offered had already been deposited in a Glasgow bank. McGinn and the board rejected his cash then.

His only previous contact with the board was back in 1972 when he had bought the rights to show live by satellite in Toronto Celtic's European Cup semi-final tie against Inter Milan – a repeat of the 1967 final which led to Celtic becoming the first British club to win the prestigious trophy. McCann negotiated the Canadian rights through Celtic director Desmond White – father of Chris White.

This time Celtic had lost 2–1. McCann had also lost. The game played at Celtic Park had gone to extra time and he had not bought enough satellite time to show the completed game.

The talks with Kelly and Smith were friendly enough but nothing positive was decided. Smith and Kelly had merely wanted to secure the support of McCann if they needed him. They thought they had got that with a promise that the exiled Scot would be the first person they would ask should they need new capital for Celtic. An expensive trip. But, thought the two directors, worth the effort.

Dempsey meanwhile had also set off across the Atlantic. His destination was New York where he was meeting up with Jim Doherty who had flown in from Toronto. Doherty was first to arrive in the Big Apple, followed a short time later by Dempsey. There was little time to get freshened up before it was back on board another aircraft. This time it was destination Bermuda to meet up with the other major financial player in the rebel camp – former carpets boss Eddie Keane. The flight down was trouble-free with Dempsey and Doherty having plenty of time to discuss the forthcoming meeting.

Back in Glasgow rivals Rangers were on their way to another cup success, beating Aberdeen at Hampden Park. The first Dempsey and Doherty knew about it was when they arrived at Bermuda. They had just walked off the plane through the heat of the day and into the terminal. After collecting their luggage they moved through to the busy concourse. It was then the voice bellowed out: 'Sorry, boys, but the Teddy Bears have won . . .' It drew only a few strange glances from those going about their business in the airport. A few – dressed in their Bermuda shorts – did pause for a second to wonder why the two men's faces fell on hearing the news. No doubt some were wondering why the two, who obviously looked like tourists, appeared to want to cry. Most people arriving on the island on a nice sunny day tend to be happy. But the significance was lost on the locals. The result, however, was soon forgotten. The Hamilton Princess Hotel was one of the biggest and best on the Caribbean island and a pleasant meal washed down with a few drinks was the perfect remedy.

Next morning the sun was beaming down from the sky. Temperatures had already risen steadily to the low seventies. Not normally the type of day for meetings, thought Dempsey. But this one was different. They ordered their cold teas outside by the swimming pool and settled down for private talks.

As the temperature rose again, this time to 76 degrees, the trio met with members of the Bermuda Celtic Supporters' Club – not a big organisation but an interested group of quite wealthy ex-pats.

On Sunday night they had dinner again to finalise their own plans. They confirmed then that there was no going back. If they didn't do something, and do something soon, they would never be able to arrest Celtic's flagging fortunes.

The next day they set off home, Doherty to Toronto and Dempsey to Glasgow. It was almost the equivalent of a full day's travel with the time difference taken into account. Having set off from Bermuda mid-morning on Monday, it was the early hours of Tuesday morning when Dempsey's flight touched down at Glasgow International Airport. A couple of hours' sleep and he was back up, showered and off to the office. That was his usual method of attempting to overcome jetlag. Stick with the local hours and quickly get into a routine.

He was quick to be briefed on events which had taken place during his short spell away. Cassidy had been having another run-in with supporters and the media about a new plan over the allocation for away match tickets. The club was to give season ticket holders priority for the away allocation. The breakaway Supporters Affiliation was threatening a boycott. Even the normally faithful official Supporters' Association had also voiced their concern. The move was seen as an attempt by the club to encourage more people to buy the expensive season tickets which gave the club cash in advance of the season – something they desperately needed.

In a letter to all supporters clubs Cassidy said Celtic had no intention of blackmailing supporters into buying season tickets. The club was also facing a backlash from the season ticket holders themselves after comments by Cassidy in the club's newspaper. Despite advertisements claiming buyers would receive 'guaranteed first opportunity to buy tickets for away games' Cassidy was quoted as saying it would not apply to the glamour games against Rangers at Ibrox. Only half the away tickets would be given to season ticket holders.

Many who had bought season tickets mainly for the Ibrox games were furious and a complaint had been lodged with the trading standards office. That was the cue for Dempsey to mix it a little. Nothing like adding a little more controversy when the board was under fire. A comment to a journalist was enough. Next day the headline was 'Celts rebel slams skinflint board'. The story continued: 'Celtic rebel Brian Dempsey has accused directors of starving the club of cash. He claimed that no shareholder has put money into the club since 1919. Yet four of the directors were taking out around £250,000 between them each year in payments.'

The comments sparked another clash with Cassidy who said: 'Dempsey has not put any money into the club either.' He claimed Michael Kelly's public relations firm was only paid around £25,000 a year and Kevin Kelly got only £5,000 as Chairman. But he refused to reveal how much was paid out to the Trophy Centre – a private firm involving Kevin Kelly and which supplied merchandise to

Celtic. He also declined to reveal how much directors Tom Grant and Chris White received for their 'jobs' at the club.

Celtic's debt was now standing at about £5 million which was causing concern – not just to the club and its bank but also to the rebels. And, there was another area of concern now filtering through to the rebels. It concerned a secret 'agreement' which had apparently been signed by five of the Celtic directors. A document which made very interesting reading.

Chapter Six

Gang of Five

Monday, 15 June 1992, 7 am.

DEMPSEY couldn't sleep. His mind had been occupied for most of the night. He had received a telephone call from a 'friend' informing him of some details contained in a document he had seen.

It referred to an agreement supposedly drawn up and signed by five Celtic directors. The same five who had closed ranks at the EGM after Dempsey and his group had blocked the removal of Grant and Farrell as directors. Grant had joined sides with the two Kellys and White after Dempsey had saved him from removal at that meeting. Smith, it appeared, made up the gang of five.

The 'agreement' had been referred to by Michael Kelly at the EGM and in a statement after the meeting read out by Chairman Kevin Kelly. At his office later that morning Dempsey found the newspaper cutting of the Chairman's comments. It quoted Kevin Kelly as saying: 'I am delighted to report that four of the major shareholders, who are also directors, have submerged their personal interests and given to each other a commitment which will achieve the long-term board-unity essential to the development of the club.' It was clear that the 'commitment' was indeed a legally binding agreement in document form.

David Low had been trying through the usual channels to obtain a copy of the document for Dempsey but without success. That, however, was about to change. Until now he had nothing tangible to go on. No registered agreement or amendment to Celtic's own company records. But, at Companies House in Edinburgh, a legal procedure was being completed.

To the young clerk going through the same old boring routine it meant nothing. Just another change of name, he thought. What he was doing was changing the name of DMWS 201 Limited, incorporated on 15 January 1992, to Celtic Nominees Limited. The new company had a registered office in Glasgow with one director . . . a Thomas Joseph Grant. Company secretary was Francis Eugene Joseph McCrossin, an accountant with Downie Wilson, who had close ties with Celtic. The registered office was in the National Bank Chambers building – the same building which housed the offices of accountants Downie Wilson. Shareholders at that stage were listed as James Kevin Kelly, Michael Kelly and David D. Smith. The authorised share capital was £100 divided into a £1 A share, a £1 B share, a £1 C share, a £1 D share and a £1 E share. There were also 95 unclassified shares of £1 each. Grant held the A share, Kevin Kelly the B share, Michael Kelly the C share and Smith the E share. Details of one share were missing at that stage but the D share belonged to Christopher White. The incorporation was now complete, the information now stored at Companies House.

It wasn't long before details of the new company were in the hands of the rebels. Low and Dempsey looked over the faxed document containing the details held at Companies House. Bingo. They could now prove the pact of five was complete and sealed.

The next stage was to get their hands on the actual document. That wasn't too long in coming and it made astonishing reading. There were 20 pages to the original draft of the pact. The first three pages dealt with the legal specifics under the heading of 'Definitions and Interpretations'. Dempsey was first to page four. He gave a slight chuckle and Low looked over.

'Listen to this,' said Dempsey and he read out the details. It contained the 'Conditions Precedent and Subsequent' which required each of the five to transfer all but ten of their personal Celtic shares into the control of the new company to the benefit of all five.

Both looked at each other in astonishment.

Low was first back to the document as if it were a race to uncover the next revelation. By page five all was becoming clear. 'Now this one is good,' chirped Low. It read: 'Under "Voting by Nominees" the five have agreed to move against any resolution calling for the removal of any one of them.' Surprise, surprise. The next section dealt with any problem arising from disagreement among the five over which way they should vote on other issues. If the five could not reach a unanimous decision on their one A, B, C, D, or E vote, then their personal share count would come into play. It meant, for example, two directors could outvote the other three if they held more shares in the club.

Then there was the question of proxy votes – where they carried the votes of shares which belonged to others. These, in the main, were relatives and friends. The pact encouraged them to obtain as many proxies as they could to be used for the benefit of all five pact members.

The five were also tied when it came to selling their shares. Under the 'Disposal' section they could only sell on condition the buyer agreed to be bound by the pact terms and on condition they informed the other pact members first. A confidentiality clause rounded off the ten-year agreement which would protect the five until 30 March –

in the year 2002. Dempsey and Low both agreed that the document had a double purpose: to protect the five directors and keep the rebels at bay. Dempsey and Low looked at each other. Both knew this would be a tough nut to crack. The main players on the board were now legally bound to each other – directors Jimmy Farrell and Jack McGinn were not party to it but they held very little shares anyway and would not pose a threat.

Low took his copy and headed back to his own city centre office. His remit now was to look at ways of challenging the pact through the courts. That was the only possible course of action as the pact appeared to put the directors' personal interests before those of Celtic Football Club. And that was not on.

The pact had proved one thing – the directors were running scared. Scared the rebels they once dismissed as 'jokers' would bring about their downfall.

So they want to keep this secret? Confidential? And already, thought Dempsey, we have a copy. So typical. So very typical. So very short-sighted.

The directors must have felt quite pleased with themselves . . . until they picked up a copy of the *Evening Times*. It didn't take the Press long to cotton on to their game plan either. The back page headline read: 'The Gang of Five Who've Carved up Celtic'. Inside the headline ran across two pages: 'Ten Year Pact to Shut Out Rebels!'. The story had all the details of the agreement and the newly formed company. It went on: 'The secret pact is one of the most important and confidential documents to emerge from Parkhead. It is in force at a time when Celtic are facing financial crisis and growing pressure over the future running of the club. They are preparing to call an AGM where accounts are expected to show them in the red to the tune of £6 million.

'The directors hope the pact will destroy any attempt by the rebels to mount an effective challenge. But the rebels

disagree and they warned that any attempt by the directors
to hide behind a pact could lead to civil action.'

Dempsey was quoted as 'a spokesman for the rebels'
and said: 'We are fully aware of this agreement between the
directors. At the end of the day the overriding
responsibility of the directors is to Celtic Football Club and
not to each other. Failure to recognise that fact carries
heavy financial penalties. They could be sued by
shareholders or creditors.'

Low was the other 'rebel spokesman'. He and Dempsey
had already agreed on what points needed highlighted.
Low's script related to the voting power. He said: 'When
you analyse the contents of this document, one thing
becomes clear. That is, both Chris White and Michael Kelly
still have control. In fact, they have even greater control.

'If the five cannot agree on an issue there is then one
vote for every one share to decide the outcome. White and
Michael Kelly have just over 4,000 shares between them.
The other three members have little over half that amount.
And because they must all go with the majority vote, it
effectively means White and Kelly can vote how they like
and the others must fall into line.'

The directors, funnily enough, were 'not available for
comment'.

It was a good attack by the rebels. The now infamous
five on the Celtic board realised the war was far from over.
It had proved to be another summer of discontent. Now
was the time to keep their heads down. Grand sermons
about Cambuslang seemed to be the only way to keep the
pressure off . . . or so they thought.

Tom Grant was sitting in his office when he agreed to
talk about work being carried out on upgrading Parkhead.
He sat in the stand, looked across to the famous 'Jungle'
and sighed. 'Cambuslang,' he said. 'We cannot build
Cambuslang tomorrow. We need things to happen quickly.
Our only option is to put more seats in here. Until we are

on the pitch at Cambuslang and kicking the ball then I will not believe it. I have always been a doubting Thomas and I will not believe it until the cash is on the table.

'We desperately want it to happen, but because of that, you tend to be blind to the pitfalls. It is everything we want in a football stadium but sometimes it is difficult to make things happen.'

The Cambuslang dream was rapidly becoming the nightmare many envisaged and Grant's words under the heading 'Pie in the Sky' didn't help. It was not a good time for the board all round. And things were about to get worse. One Terrence Cassidy was becoming a bit of a problem for them.

Several of the directors had already had a run-in or two with their chief executive. Some also believed he had been an embarrassment to the club. He spoke too often and said too much for their liking. Only four weeks before Cassidy had received a written warning from the directors after he had appeared on a television programme revealing what the board regarded as 'sensitive' negotiations over the proposed Cambuslang stadium. He had also taken over the new Family Club scheme and it was heading for disaster. Cassidy, they had decided, was heading for the dole.

The board appeared to rely on their seemingly usual sense of good timing to tell Cassidy to clear his desk. The chief executive had, only 12 hours before, enjoyed the final hours of a heady sun and gentle breeze among the white sands and palm trees of that little jewel in the Indian Ocean, Mauritius. He flew back into Glasgow on Saturday, 24 October, to be summoned to that other little jewel of the east, Celtic Park. Director Michael Kelly had requested the pleasure of his company at a meeting with a handful of other directors where Cassidy was told he was sacked. His three-year contract, worth £60,000 a year, had 14 months still to run and discussions centred on the amount of compensation Cassidy would get. Needless to say, no agreement was reached and Cassidy left for home.

He said at the time: 'I don't really want to say too much as the details of the settlement are still being negotiated. The timing might have been better, but that is the only reaction I am going to express.' He added, in his usual brash and jovial manner: 'I have no plans for the future, but, if there is anybody out there who is looking for an extremely able and successful executive, then I am available.'

Celtic issued a statement claiming the parting was a relatively friendly one. It read: 'Celtic Football Club and Terry Cassidy have mutually agreed to part company.

'The board wish to acknowledge the contribution that Mr Cassidy has made since January 1991. The board believe that a different approach to the running of the club will better meet the aspirations of Celtic.'

The following day Cassidy met several of the directors, led by White, at the offices of the club's solicitors in Glasgow. But again they failed to hammer out an agreement. The stumbling block was not the expected compensation payment – which it was believed the directors wanted to pay in instalments – but the conditions of it which related to Cassidy's silence over the more controversial highlights of his time at Celtic Park. Michael Kelly, not widely regarded as either the diplomat or an accurate predictor of future events, said the club wanted Cassidy's departure to be conducted with the minimum of fuss and free from any nastiness, unpleasantness or recourse to legal action.

Three weeks later Cassidy responded by slapping a court order on Celtic preventing them from selling their ground at Parkhead. Two sheriff officers were duly dispatched to Celtic Park with the court order. Cassidy said: 'I don't want to screw Celtic. I don't want to fight with anyone or argue with anyone. And I certainly don't want to exacerbate the situation.'

The directors might have been forgiven for thinking otherwise especially after comments from Cassidy's lawyer who said: 'The effect will be that the club will not be able to dispose of any of its heritable property. That includes the stadium. It is a step often taken where an action of damages is raised and is comparable to the arrestment of a bank account. However, there is no point in arresting an account which is overdrawn.'

The sacking and the subsequent haggling and legal moves may have astounded many fans but not Cassidy himself. He saw the boot coming and already had the shinguards on. Looking back on his departure Cassidy recalls the moment he knew he was on borrowed time. He said: 'From the day that David Smith was appointed I knew the final nail had been hammered in my coffin and relationships just went steadily downhill from there. I then had a choice. I could either say okay, what I'll do is butter up to them and make sure I keep in with all these nice and wonderful people and therefore keep my job, or I'll pursue what I believe to be the right thing to do. If I didn't that would only, sooner or later, lead me to part company with the club.

'I warned the Chairman and the rest of the directors that, in my opinion, they had made a big mistake with David Smith. And I told them an even bigger mistake they had made was getting rid of me and pinning their faith in him.

'I believe the only reason Smith remained at Celtic was because of Chris White. A lot of the directors were beginning to ask the questions I had been asking, like what had Smith done? There had been another secret meeting to appoint him as a director and at that meeting I understand Michael Kelly said to the other board members they should tell me they were about to appoint Smith at the next board meeting. He told them that if I were to find out through reading a newspaper there was going to be hell.

'So they held another secret meeting and invited me along to tell me. I said to them I assumed I was going to be appointed to the board as well. Michael Kelly and Kevin said they didn't see why not. Chris White said no.

'I asked Smith what he wanted out of Celtic Football Club. He said he didn't want to be Chairman so I asked why he insisted on being deputy Chairman. He said he felt that gave him a bit of standing.

'So I asked him again what he wanted out of Celtic Football Club. He then said he didn't want to be chief executive and he didn't want any money out of them.

'I told him he had said what he didn't want out of Celtic but not what it was he did want. Then he said he just wanted to help the club. I said to him, "Look, I've been here long enough now to run a mile when people tell me all they want to do is help Celtic Football Club." I had also been around long enough to know that no-one does nothing for nothing. I asked him again and I am still waiting for an answer.

'From that meeting onwards I knew I'd had it because I was the only one at board meetings who would actually question Smith and he couldn't afford that. My view of the directors then had got worse. If I had reported what happened at board meetings no-one would have believed me. They would have said Basil Fawlty wrote that. It is beyond belief. Nobody would believe I was dealing with people like that.

'You were dealing with a board composed of people who had achieved little in their lives. The only one you could look upon as a possible exception would be Michael Kelly because he had been Lord Provost of Glasgow. But that was not a commercial achievement it was a personal achievement.

'When I left Michael Kelly became the scapegoat. I said to Michael Kelly to watch himself because these other guys would hang him up to dry. Michael Kelly might have been considered devious but he was not dishonest.'

Cassidy then had another run-in with manager Liam Brady. The team boss had submitted an expenses claim for a trip to Leeds. Cassidy regarded it as excessive and hauled Brady into his office. Cassidy said: 'It was a figure which was fairly substantial for a trip somewhere which I knew nothing about. So I just sent it back with a comment asking him to explain what it was for. Back came the reply saying he had gone to see Leeds play and stayed overnight and Mr Farrell, one of the directors, had gone with him to study the Leeds stadium. And he explained how Mr Farrell's expenses were put on to his, Liam Brady's, Celtic American Express card. I was supposed to be the chief executive responsible for budgets and I had no idea he and Farrell were trolling off to Leeds.'

Cassidy had also pulled up Michael Kelly and David Smith for a trip to America to meet Fergus McCann and to look at stadia there. He said: 'I refused to sign their expenses amounting to some thousands of pounds and was hauled before a kangaroo court. I had already said that nobody from Celtic Football Club should be visiting America or anywhere else to look at stadia because it wasn't necessary. So not only was I not willing to sanction their expenses for that reason but secondly because I didn't even know they had gone and thirdly they had put in no report about what their findings were. We were trying to keep expenses down and keep to a budget and there was an unbudgeted expense incurred and I wasn't going to put my signature to it until I got an explanation.

'I got hauled over the coals and told that from then on all directors' expenses would go straight to Christopher White who would sanction them.

'My position within the last six months after David Smith had arrived was untenable. Towards the end of my time I viewed the board with a mixture of anger and amusement. For example, one morning Michael Kelly and David Smith came walking into my office and said, "We are the executive committee." I asked who were and they said, "We three." The two of them and me. I told them I was sorry but there wasn't an executive committee until I had been told by the board or at least the Chairman that they wanted to form an executive committee.

'I couldn't have two directors walk into my office and say an executive or any other committee has been formed. It had to be a board decision. It was farcical. At the board meeting I was told an executive committee was being formed to help the chief executive.

'I reported to the board every week and kept a daily tally of season ticket sales and we had twice as many sold than the previous best. So, bearing that in mind, Smith and Kelly turn up for the executive meeting and I ask them what they want to talk about. The first question was "How are season ticket sales going?" I just stood up and laughed. I walked round the room and couldn't stop laughing. They of course were totally insulted. Their faces were blank and you could sense the suppressed anger.

'I eventually sat down and asked if this was the level of the executive club committee activity and was I supposed to take them seriously. It was unbelievable. That, of course, was another huge nail in my coffin.'

With Cassidy out, the pact were able to get on with running things their way. But it wasn't proving easy. Kevin Kelly said they would not be replacing the chief executive, which indicated they were pinning their hopes on Smith. The flak was flying again and coming in from all angles. Kevin Kelly tried to bolster his troops with an admirable speech. 'Crisis?' he asked. 'What crisis?'

Those words led to him being torn further apart by the media. Cousin Michael Kelly decided to redress the balance. Time, he thought, for action.

Chapter Seven

Kelly's Own Goal

Thursday, 20 November 1992, Glasgow, 4 pm.

IT had been something of an adventurous day for Matt McGlone. Busy but not without its problems. Then again, he thought, the screen printing business was always fraught with colourful characters and calamities.

McGlone was 38 and lived in a tidy one-bedroom flat in Glasgow's south side. It was the ideal location for him. Close to his work, close to his friends and close enough to make the journey to Parkhead in less than 20 minutes,

He had been following the team since he was old enough to kick a ball. He had also been following with dismay the events off-the-field. It had, to him, become so much of a circus he had decided to make his feelings known. His anger and frustrations were now channelled through the satirical magazine *Once A Tim*. The fanzine had really taken off and was popular among the Celtic supporters.

McGlone had come up with the idea after the sacking of Brian Dempsey as a Celtic director. That move had been enough to motivate him into action. He now loved ridiculing the board through the pages of the fanzine – and he knew the directors had a look at it themselves if only to see what others thought of them. Not that they had to guess much anyway. McGlone had never met any of the directors personally and he had no real desire to.

The latest antics of the board and their Cambuslang 'dream' were filtering through his mind as he turned the key on the door of his flat. As usual the first thing to catch his eye as he walked inside was the flashing light on the telephone answering machine. He turned the volume up, hit the button and wandered through to the kitchen to see what delights hid inside the cupboards although not much shopping had been done that week. In the background he heard the usual hang-ups and the few messages connected with his fanzine work. He had just opened the fridge door in his search for some dinner when he heard the voice. At first he thought it was a joke but he then realised the voice was real.

'Hello Matt, it's Michael here, Michael Kelly. I wonder if you could give me a call. I have an interesting proposition for you. Thanks, bye.'

McGlone played the message again just to make sure he wasn't being duped. That, he thought, is definitely Michael Kelly. But what on earth does he want with me? And what 'interesting proposition' can he possibly have for me?

McGlone thought about the scenario for a few moments. He even considered not calling Kelly at all but his curiosity got the better of him and he picked up the telephone.

Kelly was being a real Mr Nice Guy. 'Thanks for calling back, Matt. No, I don't want to discuss it over the phone. Can you come over and see me? Tomorrow's fine, say 12 noon? Okay, thanks, I'll see you then.'

McGlone's mind was now working overtime. He couldn't for the life of him fathom out what Kelly wanted to propose. He did not sleep well that night. The following day the clock seemed to stretch the hours out longer than normal. McGlone made a telephone call to David Low. He had met the rebel member previously at a Glasgow University Celtic Supporters bash. Low, he thought, might be able to provide an insight into Kelly and what he was up to.

Certainly Low was able to supply some personal opinions on Kelly and what he was like. But even Low had no idea what the Celtic director might be up to.

At 11.30 am McGlone put his jacket on and headed into the city centre. Michael Kelly's public relations firm was in the Scottish Legal building in Bothwell Street. McGlone entered and made his way up the offices of Michael Kelly Associates. The secretary welcomed him and Kelly appeared. He ushered McGlone into his private office and opened the conversation with the line: 'Right, let's pass the buck right away. David Smith wants to do this.

'No matter what you think of the corporate board I'm sure that you will agree that the media, the coverage that we get, is absolutely horrendous.'

McGlone mumbled and nodded in agreement. But, he thought, probably no better than you deserve.

Kelly made reference to the *Evening Times* and three pages devoted to exposing the pact of five. He gave another example of the *Daily Record* with a front page picture of a man wearing a Celtic top. The man had just been convicted of a child murder. The photograph was the only one the *Record* could get their hands on but Kelly claimed the portrayal was such that 'it was as if all Celtic supporters are criminals'.

He went on: 'It's very difficult for the club to come back at the media in the way that the fans would like us to do. So David Smith had this wonderful idea that in the Christmas edition of *The Celtic View* the fanzine guys got the four inside pages and do the media.'

McGlone was glad he had switched on the tape recorder in his pocket. No-one would believe this 'proposal' otherwise.

Kelly then spoke about McGlone's fanzine, *Once a Tim*. He referred to a specific article which had ridiculed a comment made by Kelly. It came when he was asked who he was responsible to and had replied: 'I'm responsible to God I suppose.' Kelly described the mickey-take in the fanzine as 'brilliant, very clever, very intelligent'. He was still trying to justify his comment. 'It's true, it's true of any company. The directors are responsible to the shareholders and the shareholders, within the law, aren't responsible to anyone.'

McGlone interrupted: 'Well, I'm flattered by your offer but at the same time the fanzine is opposite from *The Celtic View* in that we can say what we want. If we work for *The Celtic View* it might be seen as us being sanctioned by the *View*. It might not be the image we want.'

Undaunted, Kelly persisted: 'What we need is someone to write it in that style. I'm not saying it should say these pages are written by *Once a Tim* . . .'

McGlone asked: 'You mean ghost-written?'

'Yes, if you feel uncomfortable about that then we don't say that. I don't think there's any way we can, in a conventional way, answer the press criticism without sounding tarty.

'Now, if the four pages inside were a mock combination of the *Daily Record* and *Evening Times* and they had all sorts of ludicrous stories about the paper . . . like one shows the state of the *Evening Times* financially, they're much, much worse than Celtic. So, if you did a story about that, y'know *Evening Times* collapse uhm de dum de dum, then one which says the *Evening Times* are going to charge their workers for free papers that they normally get, and you have pictures . . .'

McGlone got the picture okay: 'A mock-up idea? A direct attack on the papers in a savage fashion?'

'Yeah, but clearly seen to be done in the satirical way people know. A sort of *Private Eye* thing.'

'Interesting.' It was all McGlone could think of saying.

'Think about it.'

'I'll certainly give it a bit of thought.'

Kelly went on: 'The club itself, we don't want to be seen to be involved in this.'

I'll bet you don't, thought McGlone.

Kelly tried to settle things by changing the subject to manager Liam Brady. He told McGlone how he had to adopt a 'theatrical talent' to deal with Brady so that the manager didn't think he was interfering.

Airdrie had put Celtic out the Cup while Kelly was holidaying in Los Angeles. He referred to that, saying: 'It ruined the rest of my holiday in California. I mean, WE don't lose to Airdrie. This isn't English football where a third division side or whoever knock you out of the Cup. We don't lose to Airdrie under any circumstances and Brady hasn't twigged that.'

McGlone decided he'd had enough of this talk. 'Okay, well, I'll certainly give what you've said some thought over the weekend. Just to clarify . . . you're looking obviously for a hard-hitting attack on the slaughtering Celtic have taken, particularly in the *Daily Record* and *Evening Times*?'

'Yeah, but I think the best way to do it is, rather than defending, attacking them . . . the nasty things that the *Record* do, doorstepping people who have had tragedies, the Maxwell millions, the *Evening Times* losing money and any other nasty things you could say about journalists. They won't give it any coverage. They'll know they have been got.'

McGlone left Kelly's office hardly believing the conversation which had just taken place. He wandered out into the street and then turned off his hidden pocket tape recorder. He was glad he had decided to tape the conversation . . . just in case. He played it back several times over the weekend.

McGlone spoke about the Kelly proposition to some close friends. He also told David Low. By early on Sunday evening word had spread to a source close to the *Evening Times*. Calls were made to verify the story. When he was satisfied with the facts, George McKechnie, the newspaper's editor, dispatched a reporter and photographer to Michael Kelly's home.

It was still dark when they arrived shortly after seven am. There were no lights on in the detached stone house in the Pollokshields area of the city. The two approached the front door and the reporter rang the bell. They waited. Nothing stirred. He rang again and this time a light appeared at the top of the stairs. Through the net curtain on the glass door they saw a figure descend the stairs. It was Zeta, wife of the Celtic director.

She recognised the reporter and asked what was wrong. He told her he had to speak personally with her husband. Zeta showed them into the downstairs sitting-room and she went upstairs to inform her husband. She returned after a few minutes and asked again what the journalist wanted. Again he replied he would only convey that to Michael Kelly. Up the stairs she went again. The minutes ticked by.

The reporter and photographer were commenting on the size of the house and the furnishings when a mobile telephone rang. The photographer reached inside his pocket. 'Hello. Yes, hold on. It's for you.'

The reporter looked a little bemused. It was the news editor, Robbie Wallace. 'Where exactly are you?' he asked.

'In the Kellys' sitting-room,' was the reply.

There was laughter on the other end of the telephone.

'Well,' said Wallace, 'Michael Kelly has called his public relations man Mike Stanger. He is on the telephone to us right now. It seems Michael Kelly has called Stanger and asked him to call us to ask why you are downstairs in his house wanting to talk to him!'

The reporter tried to hold back his laughter. 'Tell him to tell Kelly to come downstairs and I'll tell him why we're here.'

It was farcical. If he shouted loud enough he could have a conversation with Kelly from the bottom of the stairs.

After another few minutes Kelly came downstairs. He had dressed in a suit, collar and tie but was still looking tired and somewhat dishevelled. He was told the early morning call was to speak to him in time for the first edition of the paper about a meeting he had had with Matt McGlone on the Friday.

'Uh, hmm . . .' was Kelly's reaction.

He was then asked if he wanted to speak about that meeting. He did not answer. When told the newspaper knew about the meeting and the contents of it he replied: 'You came here to ask me that? You had better leave. Goodbye.'

Well, thought the reporter, he had been given his chance to react and he has. But for a public relations boss one might have expected a better approach to the issue. If Kelly had laughed it off as a Christmas spoof he just might have got away with it. But his obvious embarrassment and anger appeared to prove he had sought to use the club's newspaper to ridicule the media in direct response to recent Press coverage and criticism of Celtic and its directors. Not the actions expected of a football club director and certainly not those of a man whose business relies to a certain extent on a good relationship with the media.

Once again Michael Kelly had made the front page of the *Evening Times* for the wrong reasons. 'Celtic Plot to Smear the *Times*' was the headline. The story contained all the aspects of the meeting and a detailed account of the events as they unfolded at the Kelly household that morning. McGlone had been contacted and after a bit of persuading had agreed to speak. He was quoted as saying: 'Kelly wanted the papers slaughtered the way he said they had slaughtered Celtic. Plus anything else I could think of that's nasty about journalists.

'Kelly spoke about getting over the views of the board in such a way that it didn't look as though the board was carping about the coverage.

'*The Celtic View* is simply an organ for their own rantings. If the Celtic board wish to do a hatchet job on anybody, I am sure they are capable of carrying it out themselves.'

Looking back now on that meeting, McGlone believes Kelly was both arrogant and naive to think he could have pulled off such a stunt. McGlone said: 'That meeting with him was unbelievable. His first point was to claim he liked the fanzine and thought such publications were healthy. We had already ripped him to pieces in it yet he pulled out his chequebook and said that, as he read it all the time, he should really subscribe to it and have it delivered to his home. I felt really embarrassed for him. The subscription was only six pounds a year. I told him not to bother, I would simply post him out an issue each month. I never did and never had any intention of doing so.

'When I told him I would not get involved in his plan he seemed surprised. He said we were all Celtic supporters together but I told him my venom was directed against him not against the Scottish Press. He didn't seem to grasp that fact. I regarded Michael Kelly as my arch enemy. But still he asked me to think about it and call him back.'

He did that before the *Evening Times* appeared on the Monday. But an answer to the proposal he had put on Friday was not the first thing the Celtic director wanted to know.

'Hello.'

'Hello, Michael, how are you?'

'I'm in good form . . . what's this about Peel Holdings?'

Peel Holdings, remembered Matt, was a company said to have first rights to the same Cambuslang site that Celtic said the club had for a new stadium. 'Peel Holdings? What about Peel Holdings?' asked McGlone.

'I'm asking you what is it about it.'

'What is it about it? How do you mean?'

Kelly seemed agitated. 'The Cambuslang site. I heard you were involved in some discussions about Peel Holdings.'

McGlone thought for a moment. 'I was involved? Ah, the people who do the stuff on Cambuslang for the fanzine, they know about it. They do the investigative work on that. You must have read the last fanzine.'

Kelly was even more agitated now. 'No, no, no. It was a Press inquiry today and they said that you were involved in it.'

McGlone was not sure what Kelly was getting at. 'That I'm involved in it?'

'Yeah, that you knew something about it.'

'It probably came from the fanzine, Michael. Who told you?'

'I can't disclose my sources. You'll probably read it in the paper today though.'

Matt laughed. 'Read it today? But you can't disclose your sources?'

'Certainly not.'

Well, chuckled Matt, I'll soon find out when I read who writes the article.

Kelly went on: 'As far as I know Peel Holdings have nothing to do with Celtic. Peel Holdings had an option some years ago but it lapsed. Anyway . . .'

McGlone interrupted: 'Anyway, I've been thinking about what you said on Friday. The way I see it, Michael, is, basically, my stand is that the Celtic board, including you, are not really representative of the supporters and you don't have the club's best interests at heart.'

A faint 'Uh, uh' was mumbled by Kelly.

'I don't think,' continued McGlone, 'it is what I would want to be involved in.'

'Even though you would be writing it anonymously?'

'Yes, even though I would be writing it anonymously. We are the fanzine and you are *The Celtic View* and I don't see any point in a marriage between the two.'

Kelly had stopped his 'Uh, uhs' now. It was obvious he still believed McGlone could be convinced. 'Well, I wasn't intending it to be a marriage. I think the point was that however we thought that Celtic should be run, we are both of the view that the Press are unfair to Celtic.'

'Yeah,' said McGlone. 'But we attack the board constantly and it would be futile to write for *The Celtic View*. I'm sure you can understand that. You do have an editorial staff at *The Celtic View* who can do what you're looking for.'

'Well, we'll probably do that,' said Kelly. 'It's got to be written, there's no doubt about that. It's just that you guys have developed a style of doing it . . .'

McGlone cut him short: 'We get plenty of practice!'

It worked. Kelly knew he was beaten: 'Okay, Matt, thanks for getting back so quickly. Goodbye.'

Michael Kelly was not alone in feeling 'put out'. His cousin Kevin wasn't exactly having a field day either. He had also been on the receiving end of some critical comments. A phone-in in *The Sun* newspaper revealed 90 per cent of those who called wanted rid of the Celtic board. They were joined by Canadian Jim Doherty. The rebel was speaking out again and his words were even more scathing. He dismissed the Cambuslang dream, called for Michael Kelly to go immediately and threatened another takeover showdown with the board. Chairman Kevin Kelly's response was: 'We are making progress as a club.' That comment shook even the more faithful supporters. Progress? Manager Liam Brady had already been told there was no money to spend on players as the club's overdraft continued to grow.

Celtic tried to play down the serious financial plight they had found themselves in. Their Annual General Meeting was only a few weeks away and they were trying to convince all and sundry the position was not as gloomy as many believed. Kevin Kelly had released restricted figures to the financial media and added his comments. It was a somewhat feeble attempt to take the sting out of the accounts to be presented to shareholders. Kevin Kelly had not revealed the whole extent of the club's debts.

That was a mistake and one he was about to regret.

Chapter Eight

On Account

Wednesday, 27 November 1992, 7.30 am.
Evening Times newsroom.

IT had not been a good morning. Come to think of it, it had
not been a great night either. Iain Scott was already
beginning to wish he had gone to bed earlier last night. It
was bad enough dealing with managers and footballers.
Now the sports editor had to deal with directors and
accountants.

The reporters had gone over the figures time and time
again. Yes, it could be a matter of interpretation, but the
various independent financial sources were in general
agreement. Celtic's annual accounts were confusing. Some
might even consider them downright misleading. But they
were the official figures and they did reveal the true extent
of those debts, even if it took a bit of sorting out to find
them.

The copy boys – and girls – who are the 'do everything'
people of editorial offices, had found the relevant cuttings
from previous newspapers relating to all things financial

connected with Celtic. The cuttings library staff had unearthed every bit of information from the computer system and all the data had been digested by the reporting staff. Scott was happy enough the story was accurate. So too was the newspaper's editor.

Some reaction was now being sought by those with an interest in the club but, as usual, there was a wall of silence from the Celtic directors. It was now after nine am and most of the discussions were over. The Celtic faithful were about to learn the true extent of the debts facing their club. And that was without the help or hindrance of Kevin Kelly or any of his fellow directors.

The back page looked good and the headline summed up the story perfectly: '£9 million . . . Celtic stunner as their debt almost doubles'. It was certainly a talker and a blow to the directors who thought they could present the figures their way. The report went on: 'The debts of crisis club Celtic have soared to more than £9 million. The figure will shock shareholders who were led to believe the club debt was around £5 million.' Then came the line which brought reality home to the fans. 'If forced to meet all their commitments now, the only way out would be to sell key players.'

The *Evening Times* had obtained a fully copy of the accounts. Fixed assets stood at £8.53 million and the club owed £9.05 million. That figure included nearly £5 million of an overdraft. To further boost their financial look, Celtic failed to make any allowance for depreciation of land or buildings. That fact did not escape the auditors who said Celtic should have shown an additional loss of £122,000 for that.

Another accounting move was to revalue the stadium and training ground, boosting the figure to nearly £14 million. Many believed the correct value was nearer half that amount. In addition, Celtic couldn't even sell the stadium anyway. Former chief executive Terry Cassidy had slapped a court order on the club preventing the directors from disposing of the stadium until the matter of his claimed compensation had been dealt with. And that could add another £100,000 to Celtic's debt.

An independent city analyst summed up the club's accounts, describing them as 'in a bad state'. He added: 'Technically, if the bank and creditors demanded the money due to them today, Celtic couldn't afford to pay them.'

The silence from the directors was deafening.

Brian Dempsey was sitting in his office reading the story. He had been asked for comment but had declined. Plenty of time, he thought. And he was right. The Annual General Meeting was only two weeks away and the directors would have to answer questions then.

Over at Celtic Park the pact of five were meeting to discuss their approach to the AGM. It was agreed that Smith would do most of the talking and answering of questions from shareholders. Finance was an area he could quite easily talk round. Smith and Kevin Kelly would also handle the media. Smith more so than Kelly for obvious reasons.

Meanwhile, Dempsey had managed to get up-to-date figures on shares which made interesting reading. Major changes were underway in the power structure. Vice-Chairman Smith was building a significant stake in the club. When he was confirmed as a director back in March he had no shares. The most recent list showed him with 763 and it was believed he had acquired more, taking his total to nearer 1,000. That, thought Dempsey, gives him around five per cent of the club.

Dempsey had also heard, through the usual grapevine, that Smith had bought the shares at £250 each. With the board previously approving share dealings between themselves at no more than £3.50 a share it meant someone was making a tidy little profit.

What was not known at the time was that Michael Kelly had been selling on shares to Smith. In February Kelly had increased his shareholding to 913. It had now dropped to 554. He had sold the missing 359 shares to Smith.

Several of the other directors were now becoming increasingly uneasy over Smith's growing interest in Celtic. Speculation and tension was running high as shareholders arrived for the AGM a few days later.

But the event turned out to be a bit of a damp squib. Not one of the more testing questions about directors, Cambuslang or the team were allowed. Smith effectively stage-managed the meeting and kept all questions to relevant financial matters. Even then he ducked and dived his way through tough questioning on the accounts. And he consistently refused to expand on answers to questions shareholders wanted to know.

Dempsey himself wanted to know how the directors would react to questions like: Who accepted responsibility for the financial mess? Why had five directors set up a voting pact? What is the true value of the stadium? And can the club carry on as a going concern after this season? Such questions were also parried by Smith and Kelly at the news conference after the meeting.

Dempsey was angry and frustrated. That meeting had been the first public confrontation between him and Smith. Even today he remembers that meeting and what he was told. Dempsey said: 'Smith and I had one or two heated exchanges at that meeting. I asked him to be more open with the shareholders. I accused him of not being open. We know now, having gone into the accounts, that he wasn't telling the whole story. I stressed to him at the time that if he wanted any support or goodwill he had to be open.

'He'd always claimed he'd come in as an independent director and that proved to be incorrect when Celtic Nominees Ltd, the pact, was formed. I still wanted to try and get an openness between us.

'Celtic had a mass of trade debts and in terms of the balance sheet they did owe a lot of money even to the executive club among other things. If you took all the debts together then they exceeded £9 million. There is an argument in any normal trading company that you'll always trade out of your debts but I said very quickly at that point that I didn't feel any longer that Celtic could trade out of those debts. Their turnover was only £9 million so to trade out of those debts would be virtually impossible. So the situation had become really critical from that point on and it was going to take a magical formula to take the club out of that situation. I didn't believe in magic, I only believed in a cash injection as the way out.

'Someone said, and I agreed, that the AGM had been like a party political conference with no straight answers.'

He left the meeting and headed straight home to cool off. This club, he thought, will not last much longer if things continue the way they are. He decided to speak out to the Press the next day and keep the pressure up.

This time a different tack was required. I think, thought Dempsey, we will announce that the rebels are backing down. But he had no intention of letting the Celtic board off the hook. He had something else in mind.

He waited for the telephone to ring and it wasn't long in doing so. The questions from the journalists were much the same. So too, were Dempsey's answers.

'We are backing down. There is no point in pushing the board now.' And before the startled journalists could react he qualified his comments with the punchline: 'They have got themselves into such a mess they will push themselves over the edge.

'The debt situation is the most serious situation ever to have confronted the directors. Big changes are inevitable. They are not far away and are unavoidable. We will sit back and watch it happen.'

He had, of course, no intention of sitting back.

Another Christmas was upon them but the rebels were busier than Santa Claus calling on everyone they knew who might want to sell shares. They were snapping up everything in sight. Even New Year did not provide a break with them first-footing even Kelly and White family members, albeit distant relatives. Low had made a trip to London to see some of them. They at least took the time to listen to the rebel cause but that was about as far as it progressed. Blood, as they say, is thicker than water.

But peace and goodwill were the last things on the rebels' minds as they slowly but steadily increased their shares' voting power. Dempsey recalled: 'We knew we had to step up our strength and a lot of people after that AGM, other shareholders, had become quite sickened with it all. They were confused and troubled about the future and it was important we bought up any shares on the go to strengthen our position and that's exactly what we did.

'Over that period we bought up about another eight per cent of the company. There were probably more approaches to us than we made to those shareholders. People wanted to let us know they were prepared to sell to help the cause. They were mainly smaller shareholders with 25 or 30 shares but we kept buying them up.'

The following month, February, they were in a position to start threatening again.

The first shots were fired by the rebels as Celtic stumbled again both on and off the field. On 6 February the team lost 2–0 to Falkirk, crashing out of the Cup and effectively ending their hopes for the season with three months still to run. A week later Tommy Coyne was sold to Tranmere Rovers for £350,000. But Celtic manager Liam Brady didn't get a penny – it all went towards the mounting bank overdraft.

It was at this stage that the players were beginning to feel anxious. They had been watching the off-the-field battle from the touchline. It was something alien and, to a

1990: New Celtic directors Brian Dempsey and Michael Kelly look to a better future

The two new boys are given a warm welcome by Celtic Chairman Jack McGinn

*The new team: a friendly get-together for Billy McNeill
and Terry Cassidy*

*Paradise lost: sacked manager Billy McNeill says an emotional
goodbye to one of the Celtic Park groundsmen*

New Celtic boss Liam Brady at Parkhead

Director David Smith presents the Celtic Report at the 1992 AGM

*Four just won: Colin Duncan, Matt McGlone, David Cunningham
and Brendan Sweeney at a Celtic supporters' meeting*

Kevin Kelly, Chairman of Celtic FC, and his field of dreams at Cambuslang

Say a little prayer for me: Celtic manager Lou Macari thinks of higher things at Parkhead, March 1994

Fergus McCann and Brian Dempsey emerge victorious at Parkhead, March 1994

Fergus McCann and the new board pose for photographers,
March 1994

Jubilant Celts For Change celebrate victory

Brian Dempsey and Gerald Weisfeld celebrate with the Celts For Change

Brian Dempsey is greeted at Parkhead by Jim Doherty, March 1994

certain extent, they had been protected from it. But the pressures were beginning to tell. Many of the younger team members looked to the older hands for guidance and support.

Striker Charlie Nicholas realised then the effect the Parkhead pressure pot was having on the squad. Looking back he cited the Falkirk result as a major date in the players' threatened mutiny. He remembered: 'After that game it was unanimous among the supporters and the players that there was indeed concern and it had to be expressed.

'After that Cup defeat we realised the club was in a lot of trouble at the top. Until then we had a tremendous image which was a very natural image for Celtic. A family image and a pleasant place to be. But that had lost its way. I think we have realised in Brian Dempsey the type of man we were missing. He had been at the club for a short time but his influence was tremendous. From then on there had seemed to be a separation between the team and the board.

'There were comments coming from board members like them saying through the media, "Well, we didn't lose the goals today to get beat." That is not the sort of comment you want to hear from your club directors. So it became an issue where we thought it's every man for himself. Before that we were just saying we would get on with it and play football because you really can't stand up against your employers unless it becomes so blatantly obvious things are so bad that you might get away with it, but for a long time we just had to bite our tongues and say nothing. That was hard.

'However, we knew it was only a matter of time before something broke. It had to.'

While the players struggled with their problems both on and off the football pitch, the rebels announced a top-level meeting. Twelve members of their consortium would discuss fresh takeover moves. Among them were four millionaires – Dempsey, his business partner John Keane,

Bermuda-based Eddie Keane and Michael McDonald, stepson of Gerald Weisfeld, the man who sold the What Everyone Wants chain. Their remit was to find ways to destroy the secret pact of five. They also planned to seek the support of other major shareholders and to draw up a strong financial package.

It will take time, thought Dempsey, but things are progressing for us.

While they met, cousins Michael and Kevin Kelly were serving up a double act on television. The duo appeared on Scottish Television's *Sport in Question* in front of a hostile live audience. But they took a bit of a pasting and failed to answer directly a lot of probing questions.

Asked whether the directors would step down if the right financial offer was made for control of the club, Chairman Kevin Kelly said: 'I would need to know the person and need to know if his motives were right for the club.'

Michael Kelly said: 'We would walk away from £10 million. It would have to be substantially more than that.'

Both said no financial offer had been made to the club since 1988 when Canadian millionaire Fergus McCann offered £5 million.

The rebels, of course, could counter those statements. They, through Dempsey and John Keane, had offered the club a deal which also involved prime acres at a site at Robroyston in Glasgow's north side for free. That was worth a lot of cash. And McCann had offered the club a £17 million package the previous spring – they had turned that down too.

Dempsey, however, was more intrigued by the comment from Michael Kelly that the club would be 'prepared to listen to any decent offer'. Interesting. He picked up the telephone and made a long-distance call.

'This is Fergus McCann. I'm not here right now but please leave a message.'

The sun was breaking the skies as McCann chipped a lovely eight-iron shot into the heart of the manicured ninth green. He was unaware of Dempsey leaving a message on his telephone answering machine at his Scottsdale home in Arizona. But his mind was on the same subject – Celtic.

McCann had left after the last EGM and, for a while at least, had seriously thought about forgetting all ideas concerning Celtic. But he had Celtic in his blood. Ever since his days as a committee member of the Croy Celtic Supporters Club in the early 1960s he had been one of the Bhoys. Celtic supporters are reckoned to be among the most faithful football fans in the world and it's something you don't lose easily. Even when he had emigrated to Canada the Celtic results were still looked for.

He had tried and tried hard to make the directors at Parkhead see sense. To make them believe his offers were genuine, fair and for the benefit of the club. But they were so stubborn. So steeped in their family traditions. So caught up in their own self-importance to realise that the once great and feared Glasgow Celtic were becoming second-rate citizens of the football world. No. He had decided. He couldn't walk away from it. He wanted to help and despite the attitude of the board he was willing to try once more. Dempsey he would talk to but maybe, he mused, there is another way to approach this stubborn board.

The air-conditioning in the car cooled him down as he headed back from the golf course.

The message from Dempsey was short and to the point. McCann knew there were a lot of differences to settle before he could consider joining the rebel consortium. He had already met them but the gap was too great. Both wanted to achieve the same goal but their methods were too far apart. Compromise had to be reached and McCann knew he was more stubborn than most. Some might regard it as a fault but it had done him no harm over the years. But before he travelled down that road he had one more avenue to explore. Dempsey had repeated Michael Kelly's words of being 'prepared to listen to any decent offer'.

McCann decided to take him at his word.

Chapter Nine

A Matter of Fax

Montreal, Canada. 17 June, 1993, 11 am.

THE last of the spring showers had long since gone.
Summer was now here and Canada was once more home
to Fergus McCann. He had left the scorching heat of
Arizona behind for the more acceptable climate Montreal
offered at this time of year. It was his second home. The
place he first had moved to from Scotland and where he
liked to spend the summer months. He had a nice
apartment and nice people around him here.

He had thought long and hard about the approach from
Dempsey and had spoken at length to him before leaving
Arizona. He was keen to work with Dempsey but he wasn't
so keen on some of the rebel group fighting with him.

On the flight back to Montreal McCann had read with
interest and intrigue the transcript of Michael Kelly's
comments on Scottish Television. Now, as he contemplated
the various deals he had just concluded, McCann thought
about the best way forward. It had been on his mind for

some time. A direct approach to Kelly appeared the only way.

He sat down and laid a sheet of paper in front of him. The headed notepaper had the firm Firstgreen Ltd typed in the top left-hand corner. A good name for a company about to offer a business proposition to Celtic, he thought. He wrote for about 20 minutes, addressed it to Michael Kelly at his home address, made copies to the other six directors and one to the Bank of Scotland and faxed it off to his agents in Glasgow for delivery.

It was around six pm and the sun was still shining brightly in Glasgow when there was a knock on the front door at the Kelly household. It was a hand-delivered letter for Michael Kelly.

The Celtic director eyed it with suspicion before opening it. It was headed notepaper with the words Firstgreen Ltd printed at the top and signed by Fergus McCann at the bottom. It read: 'Dear Michael, Remember when you and David Smith came to Montreal last summer and told me that if Celtic needed new capital I would be the first person you would ask? Well, since then I have been scraping my cash together, selling investments and so forth. Now that I have seen a transcript of your statements on television a few months ago, I believe I have really good news for you and the club.

'You will recall that you stated – when asked if £14 million or £20 million were offered to the club by people who showed that the traditions and goals of Celtic would be maintained but who would expect to have control of its operation – that you would have no problem accepting that.

'You also said that no-one had offered the club any money; that I had about £5 million but my local partners had pulled out.

'I am pleased to tell you that I have now raised the required cash for my plan, and it is being offered to you.

'£12.5 million has been deposited in the Bank of Scotland, or committed from me and a few other supporter partners. It forms the basis for a new capital injection of £21 million to include participation by the supporters in general and the bank.

'Michael, with the deadlines facing Celtic it's important that we get to work together on this immediately. I shall meet with you and/or your colleagues to work out the details as soon as I have your response that you indeed endorse this recapitalisation.

'I also believe that the club's supporters and creditors will want to know of this offer, so I intend to make it public very shortly.'

Kelly mulled the contents of the letter over then picked up the telephone and called fellow directors Chris White and Tom Grant. After several hours he sat down and wrote out a reply. He took it with him to his office the following day and spoke again with White and Grant.

It was ten am in Montreal and McCann had been up for a couple of hours. He was preparing to leave for a meeting when he heard the bleep and whirl of his fax machine. He stood over it as the sheets appeared. A quarter crescent moon on a dark square was at the top right corner of the paper. Below was the name Michael Kelly Associates Ltd.

When the second sheet was printed McCann lifted it and read the contents: 'Fax to Fergus McCann. Thank you for your hand-delivered letter dated 17 June 1993.

'While I have not yet had the opportunity of discussing it with all of my fellow directors (I have spoken to Chris and Tom), I am certainly interested in sitting down and discussing the details with you.

'From our point of view too, things have moved on, with Cambuslang having received planning permission and the funding package developing nicely. We have also changed the management team and appointed a club sponsor.

103

'When and where can we meet?

'Given the intense interest that Celtic arouses in the media and the disruptive effect that subsequent speculation can have, I must ask that our discussions and even the fact that we are talking again remain entirely confidential until we have reached a conclusion.

'Some weeks ago TV announced that "Fergus McCann would soon be talking to Celtic's bankers". That disturbs me.

'And before we talk I would like to know who your "few other supporter partners" are.

'I look forward to your immediate response.'

The fax ended with Kelly saying he would be in the office for the next two hours then at home and provided his home telephone number.

The fax did not exactly fill McCann with hope. In fact, quite the contrary. McCann decided a tougher tack was needed. He had a reply typed up.

The fax machine in Kelly's Glasgow office struck up the familiar notes. Out popped the reply from McCann:

'This follows your fax response and our subsequent conversation regarding my offer to refinance Celtic.

'Michael, let's keep it simple.

'Are you, subject to the details being made clear, in favour of accepting this offer of new capital as described in my letter?

'Without an affirmative answer, there is no point in meeting with you or your bankers.

'You said on the phone that you stand by your statements that I was the source of funding you favoured over other people.

'Regarding other partners, there are only two at present, both passive investors with impeccable credentials.'

McCann signed off by asking for a response by five on Monday, giving Kelly and his board the weekend to consider his offer. On the Sunday McCann received another fax but this time from his agent in Glasgow. It was a cutting from the *Sunday Mail* in Glasgow reporting that Celtic were expected to confirm their Cambuslang plans next month and that 'one of the big players in the financial package will be Fergus McCann'. It also quoted Michael Kelly saying he 'was prepared to talk to anyone who was prepared to invest real money' and added that there was no question of McCann joining the board.

McCann read it with dismay. So much for wanting to keep things confidential and not talk to the media.

The following day there was another telephone call. Celtic director David Smith. He was being exceptionally pleasant which also raised suspicions with McCann. Smith wanted to know exactly what McCann proposed and asked a lot of questions. McCann bit his lip a few times and tried as best he could to be accommodating and civil.

Four hours later the fax machine began its merry jig again. It was the reply from Kelly:

'I have had the opportunity over the weekend to consider your letter and fax and to consult those directors who are available. I also understand that David Smith has spoken to you this afternoon.

'Following that conversation, I am acutely aware that your proposal is substantially the same one that was floated last year.

'At the same time, you announced through the Press proposals to inject capital into Celtic, on certain rather unrealistic conditions. This offer was never communicated to the Celtic board except through the Press.

'Then we read that some of the conditions that you put on your offer had not been met – in particular that your proposed partners in Glasgow had failed to deliver on their financial promises.

'You then withdrew your proposals and then left Scotland, still without making any formal contact with the board.

'I would not wish this to happen again. I particularly do not want to see the efforts of our new management team undermined by fruitless speculation. Nor would I wish the excellent progress being made on the stadium and commercial front to be similarly affected adversely. Our support and all of the people who work for Celtic would like next season to begin with everyone's efforts concentrated behind the team.

'In the circumstances, therefore, I think the best course is for you to make a detailed proposal to the board, which we will consider and respond to.

'It was because of a failure of a proposal to materialise last year that I asked that the matter be kept confidential. You indicated that you wished to make things public.

'I have already faxed you a copy of an article in Saturday's *Scottish Daily Express* which refers to "secret negotiations". This did not come from me or from Celtic. The article was followed up in the *Sunday Mail*.'

The fax ended by suggesting McCann channel his cash into Cambuslang – a project McCann had already rejected.

McCann was now seething. It seemed Kelly and his board had once again failed to grasp what he was proposing. And as for the stories in the Press, well, they never originated in Montreal either.

He gave himself a few hours to cool off before writing the reply. He fed it into the fax machine and the transatlantic war of words flashed on.

Another screeched tune from the fax machine told Kelly the conflict was about to commence again. This time the machine spewed out seven pages. McCann was in a fighting mood. The first sheet was headed: 'Re £21 million new capital plan for Celtic.' It continued: 'Instead of an answer to my question, your letter of yesterday merely serves to cloud what is a clear issue. Let's try to remove some of the smoke.

'1. My offer differs from the event of a year ago in several important and substantive ways:

106

'In March 1992 I announced a plan to raise capital, requiring major participation by others which did not come about mainly because of expected opposition by you. This is now a direct offer, not just a plan.

'The required funds to proceed with it are in place and you have since publicly stated that you would "have no problem" with such a massive infusion of capital and the change in control it would lead to.

'From the known position at that time, Celtic's net debt total has worsened by £3 million and the club has incurred further losses of £3.2 million.

'This means that the offer now involves the bank.

'Additionally, of course, time is running out and it's a disgrace to see money being wasted by putting seats in the Jungle instead of a proper reconstruction project.

'2. There are no "unrealistic conditions". I did not hear any referred to last year, nor at any time since, not even in your interview nor by David Smith in his call to me when he asked questions for half an hour.

'3. "This offer was never communicated to the Celtic board except through the Press." Sorry Michael, wrong again.

'The club were promptly sent a copy of the press release.

'4. Regarding Press speculation, the sooner it is ended the better. I'm not a public relations expert but in my simple way I believe the best PR always includes doing what's best for the company and telling the truth.

'Michael, there is no point in continuing this ping-pong scenario by me making detailed proposals to your board. All this creates is more faxes going over old ground, and you raising side issues like Cambuslang commercial developments, which I don't want to hear about right now.

'I am not making formal presentations or asking for a formal signed contract from your board at this stage. I just want Michael Kelly to state a positive answer so that I can

107

meet with you in good faith and progress to the next stage without going in circles as I have in the past. If the plan has insurmountable obstacles you can spell them out then.

'This is a great opportunity for Celtic – no other British football club has had an opportunity like this. The plan, I believe, benefits all parties, from the present shareholders to the supporters and the club itself.

'I don't want to buy anyone's shares – they have little value now anyway. I want to add value by following a credible business plan.

'Please, no more long memos. Just a straight answer: Do you back this plan in principle as you said you would?

'I have to hear from you by 2 pm tomorrow.'

McCann had made his points and made them strongly. He had also included a two-page breakdown of his financial plan and a transcript of Kelly's television interview with the relevant comments highlighted.

The finance included McCann and five investors putting up £12.5 million, Celtic supporters investing £5.4 million, and loans and converted debts providing £3.1 million. It added that McCann would be chief executive with a 50 per cent stake in the club for a five-year period. After that he would sell his shares back at a discount to other shareholders.

It concluded that the overall business plan involved the rebuilding of Celtic Park at a cost of £36 million.

It was Kelly who was annoyed this time. He did not care for the tone of McCann's fax and he certainly had no intention of replying by 2 pm tomorrow.

Back in Montreal the next day McCann had just finished a light breakfast. He watched the clock strike nine and looked towards his fax machine almost imagining it rousing itself into action. But there was no bleep, buzz or whirl this time. Only silence. He knew then that Kelly would not meet the deadline.

It was at that point McCann received a telephone call

from Scotland. Another journalist wanting to know if he was still interested in Celtic. He had timed it right. McCann was in the mood for a few home truths and spoke out. After all, he did say he would go public in the interests of the club's supporters and shareholders.

Back in Glasgow the following morning Kelly was furious when he read McCann's comments detailing the offer he had put forward and claiming the directors were holding up the package. Kelly's response was immediate. Through the *Evening Times* he demanded: 'Show us the colour of your money.' And he took a swipe at McCann and the return-of-post deadline on the offer. He said: 'I can neither accept nor reject his offer until I have received much more detail. You cannot make decisions of such magnitude at short notice and certainly not by return-of-post as he initially requested.

'I have asked him to put his offer formally to the board detailing every aspect of it including the names of his associates. If he does that I am prepared to fly immediately to Montreal for a full and frank discussion of his offer.

'The truth is that we have had no time to prepare our reply properly as most of our directors are on holiday. This is the first time we have heard from him in a year and this is the same man who claimed to have a similar package deal a year ago but pulled out at the last minute.'

The article was faxed to McCann who immediately retorted with another fax to Kelly. He wrote: 'I have seen some of your statements in the Press today and if my own position is not already clear, let me try once more.

'I will meet with the directors and/or representatives of Celtic Football Club as soon as I have answers from you to two simple questions:

'Am I acceptable as someone who, in your own words, would "preserve the traditions and character of Celtic"?

'If I produced the £21 million of new capital as stated for Celtic, in your own words, "the kind of money you are talking about", will you agree in principle to accept my proposal, subject to the details being made clear and, later, formal acceptance by the Celtic board?

'I can't understand why the answer is not an immediate yes.'

McCann turned to the reference by Kelly wanting to know who the other investors were. Why, he thought, did that matter at this stage? Who was Kelly frightened of? He stuck to a straight response: 'I want to point out that my co-investors are not an issue – their credentials are excellent and their role is passive and minor. In any event any individuals unacceptable to the club could be named by you, with reasons, and I will replace their funds with my own.'

As for the other directors being 'on holiday' as the reason for Kelly not responding, he wrote: 'All your colleagues have a copy of my initial letter, but I want a reply from you showing you stand behind what you have already said. Let's get down to business. I expect your reply.'

Kelly was now losing patience. It didn't take him long to reply. McCann's fax machine burped into life once more. He plucked the message from the machine as the last letter was printed. The opening line was a little melodramatic.

'Fergus, we cannot go on faxing like this.

'I am not prepared to conduct our discussions through the media. When it is ready, put your detailed plan to the board. We will consider it and respond.'

McCann responded with equal haste. 'I agree the faxes and publicity, made necessary by your continued failure to give an answer, must end.

'They will and we will arrange to meet privately, as soon as you state whether I and my money, which would put me in a 50 per cent position, are acceptable or not.

'With all the risk I am taking, I should be the one to be asking questions in advance. Let me have a direct answer by 12 noon tomorrow.'

McCann's fax machine sat silently in a corner as the deadline passed.

Four days later, after an approach by McCann through his Glasgow agents, Kelly said he had considered with the other directors an offer to meet with McCann but saw no benefit in such a meeting at that stage.

It was to be a big mistake. McCann was now about to form one of the most powerful partnerships ever to challenge the Celtic family dynasties.

Chapter Ten

The Old Firm?

Glasgow, Thursday, 1 July 1993.

IT had been almost a week now since McCann and Kelly had fought out their transatlantic battle of words. McCann had thought long and hard about the offer and Celtic's seemingly brick-walled approach. Even an offer of talks from Kevin Kelly fell flat 24 hours later when the Chairman cancelled the meeting.

Now David Low had been in touch through McCann's agents in Glasgow. It was time he started talking to Dempsey and his crew once more. Sending two ships into battle without co-ordination was not how the war would be won. It was back to a joint approach. This, it would seem, would be the only sensible way to achieve the end. But it would have to be done on McCann's terms – or at least with a lot of his influence.

McCann now had his financial advisers at Pannell Kerr Forster in Glasgow working with city public relations firm Barkers. Through them he released a Press statement revealing he was not willing to waste any more time on the matter. The strongly worded statement concluded: 'Press manipulation, avoidance, stalling, personal attacks, hiding behind a series of directors' upcoming holidays, are not the way to do business when so much is at stake and the urgency so great.

'I'm not interested in playing games. I can only conclude that the answer from Celtic is no.

'This is clear whatever the offer, whoever the source, no matter what they say publicly.

'No matter how beneficial for the club, the personal agendas for the directors obviously matter more.

'Accordingly I have decided not to waste any further time and money and have today withdrawn my offer and the money that goes with it.'

Further details were also revealed to the media, including a statement that McCann had been falsely linked as an investor for Cambuslang and not the club. McCann believed that information had come from Michael Kelly. The Glasgow public relations man and Celtic director responded on behalf of the club, saying of McCann: 'No reasonable person would expect that serious progress could have been made by transatlantic fax and press statements. It was another offer which never was.'

McCann may not have been happy with Kelly's statement but he knew it would be futile to engage the Celtic spokesman in further conversation. Better let him believe what he does, thought McCann. It was a good tactic and would allow McCann to build on the talks with Dempsey without attracting too much attention. McCann might be considered a bit of a terrier when it came to business but that was how he had made his money. He had made mistakes but they were becoming fewer as the years rolled on.

Dempsey, meanwhile, had been pulling various interested parties together. His main team included the two

Keanes, Weisfeld and Doherty. Weisfeld was probably the less enthusiastic of the group. He, believed Dempsey, really appeared to want to do his own thing. But with McCann now willing to boost their ranks, Dempsey thought it would be a good idea for all of them to get together.

But Dempsey knew there was one possible stumbling block and that was the mixing of McCann and Weisfeld. A difficult combination, thought Dempsey, both self-made millionaires with different approaches to the Celtic challenge.

McCann was still of the opinion the battle should be fought by the American rules. He wanted to set up a parallel company with millions in a bank account and wait for the bank to move against Celtic, call in their loans and invite the new firm to get involved. That would give McCann what he wanted – complete control.

It was effectively, a vulture-like approach. It worked well in the United States but Dempsey and Weisfeld thought it was the wrong approach for Scotland. There were too many avenues of escape for the Celtic board and they could hold on for too long. Dempsey wanted a straightforward legal approach to out-vote the directors and get support for a new share issue. Weisfeld was of a similar mind and he also wanted overall control.

Dempsey decided to test the water and invited both millionaires to meet. The venue was the Glasgow offices of solicitors Maclay, Murray and Spens in St Vincent Street. Dempsey and McCann arrived first and were shown into the boardroom. It was a big room. Long and with enough seating for 24 people. McCann looked around then chose to walk to the furthest away part of the room and sit at the head of the table. Within minutes Weisfeld arrived. He walked into the boardroom. McCann stood up but made no attempt to bridge the ground between them. Weisfeld made the long walk to the other end of the table and shook McCann's hand. McCann asked: 'Do you want to join OUR plan?' He made it clear it was the parallel company approach he was referring to.

Weisfeld replied: 'I don't think your plan will work.'

McCann looked at him and said bluntly: 'Then I think we are wasting each other's time.'

Weisfeld said goodbye, shook McCann's hand again and promptly left. It was a sign of a clash of egos and the start of a parting of company between Weisfeld and the others with Dempsey deciding to side with McCann.

Dempsey said of that period: 'I asked David Low to contact Fergus and his advisors and start thrashing out a deal. I was prepared to compromise a great many things because I felt instinctively that the situation at Celtic was now irretrievable and we had to have an alternative lined up which would be meaningful and substantial.

'The meetings began in earnest in August and by September we had virtually agreed the way forward. It wasn't difficult. All I wanted to do was ensure that, at the end of the day, Fergus would sell his shares back to the supporters as he had promised to do after five years in charge. And, at the beginning of the day, there would be shares available for the supporters. Those were the only two points I really wanted to stick on and that wasn't a problem with the man.

'The talks were very cordial, very happy, very productive and constructive. I don't think anyone else shared my feeling that the situation at Celtic was becoming irretrievable but the talks started to point in that direction.

'The real difference in our approach was the way forward. Fergus was insisting on the parallel approach and we wanted to go straight into the EGM route with the shareholders. We had to convince him that our way was better and eventually we did that by convincing his advisers first and letting them convince him. He was quite adamant and so, at stage, were his advisors but they were eventually converted to our way forward.'

Dempsey felt happier. He could see a stronger and clearer way forward now. He and McCann had agreed to go public with their new 'team'.

Shortly before three pm on 24 September, the media started to arrive at the offices of Pannell Kerr Forster. They crushed into the boardroom and when it seemed no-one else could conceivably enter the small room, in trotted McCann, Dempsey and Dominic Keane. They took their seats and Dempsey introduced the three amid the clicking and flashing from a battery of cameras.

He revealed a £20 million package to save Celtic. It consisted of £12.5 million from McCann and £1 million each from Dempsey, his partner John Keane, Canadian financier and friend of McCann, Albert Friedberg, and Eddie Keane who was represented by his brother Dominic. A further £2 million would be loaned to Celtic by McCann with the remaining £5.4 million coming from the issue of new shares.

Dempsey continued: 'Myself and the other Scottish investors are united with Fergus in this project. I have consistently said that this investment plan is the best way forward. Now that plan is bigger and better than ever before and Celtic's need for it is even greater. Although we want to help the club, I want to stress this money is not a donation. We believe Fergus's ambitious goals for Celtic can be achieved both on the field and on the balance sheet. We have made these commitments as long-term investors.'

McCann added: 'I want to consult with shareholders and obtain their support. And I intend to communicate directly with the thousands of supporters who have written to me or responded to my questionnaire asking if they would invest in new shares. The response has been both very heavy and very positive. They are anxious for change, they want to back my plan and they believe, like me, that Celtic requires new capital and improved management.'

The rebels were now united, the old firm of Dempsey and McCann were back in business and pressure was about to be heaped on to the Celtic board.

As if they didn't have enough of that already with things not going well once again on the park. Just as McCann and Dempsey appeared in unity Celtic lost 1–0 to old firm rivals Rangers at Ibrox in the League Cup semi-final. The new season had got off to another bad start and the fans were getting even more restless. Executive box holders, season ticket holders, even the ordinary travelling support were now calling for change and booing both the directors and the team. Manager Liam Brady was also now feeling the pressure. It was not the situation he had either expected or enjoyed.

Four weeks later Celtic took on St Johnstone at McDiarmid Park, Perth. The final seconds ticked away and Celtic were on their way to another defeat. Michael Kelly sat stone-faced as the referee's whistle brought the match to a close. St Johnstone had won 2–1. Kelly rose from his seat in the directors' box and headed towards the lounge. He had only walked a few steps when he felt a hard slap on his back. He spun round to be confronted by a Celtic supporter who glowered at Kelly and said with more than a hint of sarcasm: 'How about that then, Michael? Are you happy with the club?'

Kelly saw red. He flew into a rage, shouting at the man and calling for the police. He threatened the Glasgow businessman, financial adviser and long-time Cetic fan Brian McKenna, saying he would have him charged with assault. Other directors, including those from St Johnstone, were clearly embarrassed. They ushered Kelly away as he shouted: 'I want his name!'

The outburst also took McKenna by surprise. He said: 'He over-reacted. The whole thing is absolutely ridiculous. If Michael Kelly cannot take a bit of verbal criticism he should not be at the club.'

Back in the lounge Kelly was calmed down. He was persuaded not to press charges.

The incident reflected the pressure and tension Kelly and his fellow directors were feeling. In addition to everything else the plans for the Cambuslang stadium were way behind schedule. The man trying to raise cash for the project was Pat Nally. His previous firm, Chelsea Promotions, of which he was sole director, was deep in debt. The normally faithful Celtic Supporters Association – who had stuck with the board through thick and thin – had shocked the directors only three days earlier by delivering a unanimous vote of no confidence in the board.

And the court action by Terry Cassidy was looming. The directors had met to discuss Cassidy and had decided to counter-claim that the former chief executive was guilty of gross industrial misconduct. Kelly hoped that the counterclaim would be successful.

The next set of annual accounts were also due that week and a lot of work was being put into the presentation of them. The directors just had to make them look better this time.

But if Michael Kelly and his fellow directors had plenty to hinder their sleep that night, there was a bigger nightmare to face in the morning.

As the sun rose over Parkhead and the reality of dropping to ninth place in the league dawned, Liam Brady quit. The Celtic manager had had enough. After the defeat by St Johnstone, Brady could face the failure no more. He offered his resignation to Chairman Kevin Kelly and it was accepted. His decision to quit was no real shock to those who knew him. He too had been under pressure in the hot seat at the club which was never out of the headlines for the wrong reasons. Despite his great promises Celtic, under his two-and-a-half-year reign, had failed to win a trophy.

Brady himself realised the pressures the entire club was facing when he announced his decision. He said: 'The board, the staff, the players and the supporters are feeling it. It was my responsibility to lift the players and, when I found I was unable to do so, I felt it was time to stand down.'

Kevin Kelly then spoke the memorable words: 'He has done the honourable thing in resigning.'

Brady's right-hand man, Joe Jordan, took over the helm. The AGM was only another day away and this latest blow was obviously going to add to the fireworks.

On top of this Celtic were due to meet Sporting Lisbon in the UEFA Cup in less then two weeks' time. The point wasn't lost on one Alberto da Silva from the Lisbon newspaper *A Dola*. He had arrived at Parkhead to see the team leave for the St Johnstone match. He had wanted to interview the 'manager Mr Brady'. He had been told to return the following day. Now he stood among a group of Scottish reporters and, as a chill wind turned his face a nice shade of blue, he stuttered in broken English: 'Where I see Mr Brady? I have interview with Mr Brady . . .' He was told Mr Brady was no longer manager. 'Who manager?' he asked.

'You must speak to Joe Jordan, he is the manager,' came the reply. Alberto, all five feet of him and wrapped in a massive sheepskin, headed for the main reception at Celtic Park.

The next day the Scottish media was full of the 'Brady Quits' headlines. He, as most managers do when they leave a club without success, received the usual scathing attacks, some constructive criticism and the odd helping of sympathy. Speculation also covered the papers as to who the new boss would be. Would Joe Jordan survive?

No, was the quick answer. Jordan quit that day – just 24 hours after Brady. Jordan revealed that he had made a pact to go if Brady quit the club. He said Brady's departure had forced him to leave on a point of principle.

The sensational announcement by the caretaker boss plunged the crisis-hit club into further turmoil. Again the media swarmed into Celtic Park. Again the bitter wind blew. Again a bewildered Alberto da Silva arrived. 'I here to interview manager Mr Jordan,' he said, rather proud of his pronunciation. He was told Mr Jordan was no longer manager of Celtic. 'Who manager today?' he asked.

'You must speak to Frank Connor, he is the manager,' came the reply.

Poor Alberto rolled his eyes to the heavens and mumbled: 'Who tell my editor? My editor want to know how many managers Celtic have? Why they have new manager every day?' He never did get his interview.

But as Alberto walked off in shock, so too did the Celtic fans. George Delaney of the Celtic Supporters Association described it as 'a bit of a blow. He says he's going on a point of principle. It's so nice to see a guy in football have principles.' Asked if he felt the same should apply to the board he added: 'You won't get me to comment on that.' Dempsey did. He said: 'Celtic was once a great club, now it is falling apart at the seams. Something has to happen quickly to stabilise this club and it must come from the top. Changes have to be made on the board. A lot of people are doing the "honourable" thing at Parkhead. I would like to see the directors do the same.'

Feelings were understandably running high as shareholders arrived for the annual general meeting later that day.

Dempsey, McCann and Doherty were there but they knew it was a bit of a lost cause. The directors had enough of the votes to control the meeting and they were not in the mood to be questioned about issues other than those concerning the agenda and that related mainly to the annual accounts. It was a stormy meeting and a long one but the directors managed to emerge unscathed although leaving a lot of unanswered questions behind.

The board survive again, thought Dempsey, but they have the most powerful adversary yet to face. The McCann and Dempsey consortium was still jockeying for position before making the first real moves in the next assault . . . the extraordinary general meeting successfully sought by the rebels and due in five weeks' time. Doherty was by now beginning to take a back seat to 'let the boys with the real money get on with the job'.

And that they did.

McCann was now staying in Glasgow for the next month. His presence was needed to see through the EGM and the run-up to it. All was relatively quiet on the Parkhead front for the next week and even the team seemed to respond to the respite, beating Sporting Lisbon 1–0 in the first leg of their UEFA Cup tie at Parkhead. But a one-goal lead was a little precarious – whether you be a player on the field or off . . .

The rebels were now stepping up a gear and contacting all the shareholders they could. That included relatives of the White, Kelly and Grant families. McCann by now had become quietly confident he was going to swing things his way. Dempsey wasn't so sure.

McCann had organised off-the-record press briefings for journalists to keep them informed and to keep the pressure up on the board. He had a lot to say and fed it well at appropriate intervals. A lot of his information related to what other people had said or were doing. But he also possessed interesting facts and figures not widely known – and he knew that. Within weeks he had the media rushing about chasing all sorts of stories to keep the issue alive.

He then fed the media certain information about the contacting of directors' reatives. 'Come and join us' was the typical headline as McCann and his team got the bandwagon going. The rebels had visited and tried to persuade the White and Kelly family connections in London to switch sides. McCann was quoted as saying: 'The present board own 40 per cent of the voting shares. A total of 18 per cent is owned by family or friends who now hold the future of the club in their hands. With their support we can restore glory to Celtic.'

As the public war of words continued, Celtic directors plucked Stoke City manager and former Celtic player Lou Macari and named him as the new team manager. During the first 90 years of Celtic Football Club there were just four managers. Since the legendary Stein era ended, five managers have been appointed to one of the hottest seats in football. Macari was the latest in that line.

During 15 troubled years for managers at Parkhead the names and faces in the boardroom have seldom changed. It has always been the men who faced the big challenge on the field who carried the can. Now Macari, the man who in 93 games had grabbed 58 goals for Celtic in the 60s and 70s, was the promised 'saviour' of Celtic. The man who would take them to further glory. But the fans were not convinced.

Chapter Eleven

Back the Team

Stoke, Friday, 21 October 1993, 9.30 am.

IT had been a long day and a long night for Celtic director David Smith. But it had been worth it. After two weeks of tough talking, the board at Stoke City had finally bowed to the inevitable. The club had given the green light for Celtic to approach Stoke manager Lou Macari and talk to him about the Parkhead job. Initially Stoke wanted a massive £500,000 agreed in compensation before allowing Celtic to formally offer Macari the manager's job. But that figure had been reduced to just over £100,000, clearing the way for Smith to talk terms. Those talks had gone well and they would meet again to finalise the contract and agree the salary.

Macari knew the problems at Celtic Park, both on the field and off it. But he had no hesitation in saying yes. Celtic had no match today and his first game as manager would be a big one . . . old firm rivals Rangers at Ibrox. Celtic Chairman Kevin Kelly was in no rush to announce the appointment of a new manager. He was waiting for confirmation from Smith that everything had been signed and sealed.

Four days later his wish was granted and Macari returned to Parkhead 20 years after he had been transferred to Manchester United. He knew he had arrived amid troubled times but he was no stranger to controversy. He had already been censured and fined £1,000 following a betting scandal while he was manager of Swindon. A large bet had been placed on the club losing a Cup tie to Newcastle United. Swindon lost 5–0. The FA ruled Macari's involvement was minimal but still felt he should be punished. He was also taken to court accused of a tax fiddle involving under-the-counter payments to Swindon players but he won his case and was cleared.

Macari breezed into Celtic Park as the rebels who wanted to become his new bosses at the club continued to buy up proxy votes. Dempsey and McCann watched the soap opera unfold and then enjoyed another bit of drama as Celtic headed for Ibrox and then emerged with a 2–1 victory for their new team boss.

Macari was delighted. The win had been something he had hoped for but really didn't expect. His first after-match news conference was sweet. He said: 'We're not going to kid ourselves that, after just one Old Firm win, we are on the road to great things. But with a European tie on the agenda this midweek there is no doubt it is a great boost to everyone connected with the club.'

Macari's delight was obvious but that of the beleaguered directors was even more so. At last they had something to smile about. But not for long.

Four days later, on a cool evening at the Jose Alvalade stadium, Macari looked at the youngsters on his substitutes bench, two 19-year-olds, a 21-year-old and another barely a year older, and admitted he was frightened. The three-foreigners ruling meant he had to do without three of his more talented players – Polish international skipper Dariuz Wdowczyk, striker Andy Payton and Albanian international defender Rudi Vata. Just over 70 minutes later his fears were confirmed as Celtic went out of Europe, beaten 2–0 on the night and 2–1 on aggregate.

Macari knew then he needed money for new players at Celtic. But cash was tight. The club had massive debts and even dumping some of the players to pull money in would be difficult. Basically, the first team players were on salaries which would scare off other clubs. Macari had been stunned when he discovered just how much some of the Celtic stars were getting paid – and he said so. He revealed that was a big stumbling block to his rebuilding plans. It had already been made clear to him in no uncertain terms by the directors that he must sell before he could buy. It was yet another example of questionable management of money at Celtic Park. Macari said: 'If I was to try to do a swap deal with any English club the first thing their chairman would ask is: "How much is your lad on?" When I tell them they would say: "Bloody hell. I can't afford that."'

His comments and the attitude of the directors were the final straw for many fans. Success on the park was all they were interested in. Fanzine author Matt McGlone was among these who had decided to distribute leaflets outside Celtic Park for the game with Partick Thistle – Macari's first home game in charge. A rally was called and 10,000 leaflets were handed out calling for the resignation of the directors. The slogan 'Sack the Board' had been born.

Macari tried to quell the rebellion just hours before the match against Thistle. He pleaded: 'I would like to think that everyone who turns up today will be here simply to support the players. I don't want any distractions or for the players to come off the field and say the crowd reaction got to them. It is the fans who generate the cash for managers to go out and spend on players and we need them to come here in numbers.'

The fans listened and sympathised but they had had enough. The demonstration against the board went ahead regardless.

Dempsey spent the Sunday morning relaxing at home, reading the match report and noting with great interest the groundswell of anti-board feeling now manifesting itself at Celtic Park. Time, he thought, to stir things a little more and keep the pot boiling. He then revealed, during one of his many daily conversations with reporters, that the rebel consortium had £5 million sitting there for Macari to buy new players. Without the backing of McCann and Dempsey his buying power was virtually zero. The rebels had already deposited £12.5 million with Celtic's bankers, the Bank of Scotland. Dempsey vowed: 'The cash is there. The most important part of our plan is to bring success back to Celtic Football Club. The board know the cash is there and it is up to them to take it . . . provided they hand over control of the boardroom. The fans have already told the board what they want and that was obvious after the demo outside Parkhead. Macari has told the board what he wants and needs but the directors are burying their heads in the sand. We sense a degree of friction already building up between him and the board. It must be very frustrating for him to know the money is there to buy any player in Britain but his board will not give him access to it.'

Macari read the words and cursed the problems preventing him getting his hands on the cash. But there was little he could do at that stage. The crucial Extraordinary General Meeting was now only three weeks away. That could change everything for Macari – or plunge matters further into chaos.

Meanwhile, Macari's warnings about not being able to unload top earners had just been proved right. After reading Dempsey's comments he got a call from

Middlesbrough. The English First Division side had shown an interest in the return of their former hero Tony Mowbray. Liam Brady had bought the central defender for £1 million two years ago. But Middlesbrough were not happy with the £600,000 asking fee from Macari and when they then learned of the player's personal terms they withdrew.

Macari, however, was managing to keep things together on the field. He now had a seven-game unbeaten record since taking over and had only dropped two points – one to Aberdeen and then another to Kilmarnock.

But the biggest struggle was that happening off-the-ball. The rebels launched a legal fight to try to end the infamous pact of five. The shock move was to be heard at the Court of Session in Edinburgh the day before the EGM. Both sides had lawyers scurrying around.

Even the fans were squaring up to each other. In one corner was McGlone – representing a now growing majority of those opposed to the board. In the other was Gerry McSherry – one of a small number of supporters who actually spoke up on behalf of the board. Forty-one-year-old McSherry had effectively been fighting a one-man crusade for a continued Celtic family dynasty.

He had watched dismayed as the board faced broadside after broadside over their handling of the club. And he had fought back on their behalf – speaking out when directors refused and even when they did. He blasted: 'To let the businessmen take over the running of the club will mean the end of Celtic traditions. I have every confidence in the directors. Things will come good for Celtic and money will appear. It is a problem facing all football clubs just now. It is farcical the stuff that's been coming from the rebel camp. For three years we have been drip-fed with Celtic-board-in-crisis stuff. Brian Dempsey merely wants to appear on a big white horse as the saviour of Celtic. Fergus McCann is simply an innocent abroad being used by the rebels and he will wise up sooner or later.

The cash will flow into Celtic once they move to Cambuslang. Things are looking fantastic for the club under the present family control and nothing is going to change that. The rebels are finished.'

But McGlone hit back: 'The rebels are men of vision, business acumen and, more importantly, have money. They are also Celtic supporters who are genuinely worried about the state of the club. To ignore an offer like this is ludicrous. I don't think Cambuslang will happen. The money isn't really there. For years the board have ignored the club financially. It has all been take with them. If the board do not go it will be doomsday for Celtic. I believe the rebels will eventually win. Resistance will grow if the board insist on hanging on.'

Celtic Chairman Kevin Kelly was next on the public podium. He sent a letter to shareholders calling on them to back the board. He claimed the rebels' plan to issue new shares would value the club at just £1.2 million and added: 'I am sure I am not the only person who believes Celtic Football Club is worth more than that. I do not think it is over-optimistic for me to suggest that our first team pool would realistically be valued at £8 to £10 million.' But he later conceded the transfer value of players was not included as part of the club's balance sheet. In his letter he hit out at 'misinformation' surrounding the club and said: 'It is difficult to avoid the conclusion that a deliberate campaign to undermine the club has been taking place.' He denied that the club was turning its back on the problem and said that 'in difficult times' any business would consider raising further capital. But he did not see the rebel offer as the answer.

Dempsey responded by rejecting suggestions of a deliberate campaign to undermine the club. He said: 'On the contrary, we are trying to put millions in to help the club. This is the biggest financial rescue in British soccer history. How can this be undermining the club?'

But the biggest swipe at Kelly's letter and comments came from within. As the rebels fought their case against the pact of five in court, Celtic director Jimmy Farrell – who was not a pact member – was sending out a statement. The club's longest-serving director sensationally climbed on board with the rebels. He told shareholders the very survival of the club would be at risk if fresh capital was not found. Solicitor Farrell chose his moment carefully. In his statement to shareholders he said: 'You will have received a circular letter from your chairman and noticed that he offers no guidance to you on the current proposals. Neither does he propose any alternative solution to the company's pressing financial problems. The company is in massive financial difficulty and an increase in share capital is necessary to ensure its very survival. We have before us a very real offer of increased share capital from the Fergus McCann consortium. I strongly urge you to support the resolutions before this EGM.' Farrell held little in terms of share votes but his family count came to around 5.5 per cent of the total shareholders' votes. His shock statement was to be only one of several during the next 24 hours.

Back at the Court of Session things were not going the rebels' way. The main action on behalf of the shareholders had been launched by elderly Betty Devlin – the widow of former Celtic Chairman Tom Devlin. She was seeking an order to ban the pact of five from voting at the EGM the next night. The judge, Lord Sutherland, heard claims by the shareholders that Celtic would quickly become insolvent without an injection of fresh capital such as that on offer from the rebel consortium. But a two-thirds majority was needed to approve that and the pact had more than enough voting power to prevent that happening which would not be in the interests of the club.

Both the rebels and the club had hired Queen's Counsel for the case. William Nimmo Smith for the rebels argued: 'The pact could serve no other purpose than the

129

maintenance of these five individuals in their position as directors.'

But Neil Davidson for the club said: 'The company is improving its financial performance. The assumption that Celtic are inevitably tumbling towards insolvency is wholly unfounded.'

McCann was in court to hear Lord Sutherland kick the legal effort by the consortium into touch. The judge refused to grant the order against the pact, saying the information before him did not satisfy him that Celtic were in immediate danger of insolvency and collapse.

McCann left the court with his head hung low. He said: 'I feel very badly. The club will decline to a very sorry state rather than disappear overnight. But there is no way I could come back and deal with this board. I will not invest in Celtic under the present control.' The rebels seemed resigned now to a quick EGM with the pact wiping them away. Dempsey and McCann spoke little that night. There seemed no point in having lengthy talks about a foregone conclusion.

But the next morning there was an unexpected boost in defeat. Celtic director and pact member Tom Grant had also thrown his weight behind the rebels. Despite the legal failure which meant certain defeat at the EGM, the switch by Grant put the rebels on a high. Grant could not break the pact and must vote with them at the meeting but his views would help the cause and further embarrass the other four pact members. The pressure on them from the fans and the board would also increase. Grant spoke out to the *Evening Times*, saying a compromise should be sought over the future of Celtic. He said: 'I can't change the vote tonight. But there is still room for compromise. I feel that now the pact has been declared legal and not a threat to the club we should disband it as a goodwill gesture. It was not the spirit of the agreement to vote against Celtic.'

Grant, Celtic's stadium director, also confirmed his earlier views that Cambuslang would not happen. He said:

'I would be surprised if it did and not entirely disappointed if it doesn't. We have never been told where the funding is coming from. Our consultants, Superstadia, had said they would tell us in a few days who was underwriting the £20 million for the stadium. It never happened. I feel most of our fans want to watch Celtic at Celtic Park.'

Grant had already been threatened with removal from his job before but he said he had told his fellow directors of his views. They also could not sack Grant as a director because of the pact. He added: 'If Fergus McCann pulls out of his takeover bid I will be disappointed. I do not know what the future is because I do not know what the other directors want to do. But I am upset because the fans must be viewing this with total confusion. There are a lot of good things in Fergus McCann's proposals but there are also a lot of things which are not. However, I believe there is room for compromise.'

Dempsey appreciated the stand and the comments but he knew they would change little. He said: 'The only people who will not be in that room tonight are the two who matter – the bank and the fans. We fully expect to lose our case but we will make our voice heard.' And make their voice heard they did.

So too did the Celtic support. Hundreds of fans chanted outside the ground as shareholders arrived for the meeting. More than 200 of them shouted slogans against the board. The fierce debate over the future of the club resulted in a lot of thin answers from the board during the four-hour meeting. Eventually a show of hands was all the pact needed to win the night. The bid for control and McCann and Dempsey's money ended in a tie with 47 votes each. But it was well short of the two-thirds majority the rebels needed.

McCann and Dempsey left the meeting exhausted. They were met with cheers outside. McCann headed off into the darkness. He wanted to be back in the heat of Arizona where he spent his winters, not here in a cold and damp Glasgow with the pain of defeat fresh. Dempsey took time to tell his supporters: 'Thank you, but there is no way forward for us now. We have tried legally, financially, emotionally and I regret we have failed.' He too then trudged off home.

Chapter Twelve

Bhoys' Own Story

Saturday, 27 November 1993.
Celtic Park, 3.15 pm.

MATT McGLONE was cold, wet and miserable. The heavens had opened up and he knew it was going to be another day of getting soaked to the skin. He wondered why he did this week in, week out, especially for a game against Raith Rovers and the day after the Celtic board had rejected a life-saving £18 million. He looked around at the other faces beside him. They seemed to be of the same opinion, judging by the expression on their faces. Out of the corner of his eye he saw a small figure approach him. He had seen the same chap talking to several others within the terracing. Now he had sidled up to McGlone.

'Matt McGlone?'

'Yeah.'

'Brendan Sweeney . . . what did you make of last night's meeting then?' It didn't take much to get McGlone talking about Celtic and even less to encourage some scathing remarks about the board. He and Sweeney quickly became good friends. More than that, they agreed there was a need for change at Celtic Park and believed that if McCann and Dempsey were going to walk away then the fans themselves had to do something. It was the birth of the Celts for Change group . . . the fans who decided action went hand-in-hand with words and were not afraid to rally to the call. The larger Affiliation of Celtic Supporters' Clubs, led by Paisley promotions man Peter Rafferty, had been involved in plenty of talk so far but no real action. They were regarded until then as the only alternative to the more sedate and official Celtic Supporters Association. Both the larger groups each had around 12,000 members. The Celts for Change group was small indeed by comparison.

During the first couple of meetings that same week McGlone, Sweeney and a handful of others chose to meet in their own homes or in pubs. For their first 'come along anyone who is interested' meeting they hired a 50-seat room in Glasgow City Halls. The leaders were quite nervous as the time of the meeting approached, wondering if anyone would show. They didn't wait long. The room was quickly changed for a larger one when 450 people turned up. McGlone and Sweeney were delighted. At last they could see change. The supporters were reacting and the strength of feeling against the board was growing. Govan Town Hall was the next venue, on 9 December, but even that venue, with its capacity of 950, was stretched.

By now even the board were wondering if change would have to come to quell the rising anger being directed at them. Speculation grew that Michael Kelly was under pressure to resign from some directors who saw his departure as one way of calming the situation and reversing falling attendances at home games.

Celts for Change had already succeeded in encouraging most fans to stay away from the Rangers end of the stadium for the visit of St Johnstone. In their place they took a banner reading: 'Back the team, sack the board'. The group had also organised a protest outside the Bank of Scotland branch in the city centre in protest at the bank's refusal to intervene after McCann and Dempsey offered the £18 million package. Crowds at Celtic Park were continuing to fall well below the 20,000 mark and financially it was hurting the club.

Dempsey viewed the developments with interest. He had not expected quite such a surge in support for change so quickly. It was not long before the telephone was ringing again in Scottsdale, Arizona. McCann and Dempsey spoke several times before Christmas. Dempsey was still reluctant to return to the ring so soon after the points decision went against them. McCann, however, was eager once more to return to the fray. He didn't like losing and he especially didn't like losing to the directors who made up the board at Celtic Park. At times Dempsey had to convince McCann not to jump on the first available plane back to Glasgow with his sleeves rolled up and his cap turned round.

A boycott was the action now being called for by the Celts for Change members. The committee were trying to resist that. They wanted to try to convince the other supporters' bodies to join them first. In the short term they proposed the board give the fans a say in the running of the club, boycott Celtic products and picket the homes of directors. Around 400 members had pledged not to renew their season tickets and 25 Celtic supporters' clubs in Northern Ireland vowed to stay away from Parkhead until the board were removed.

McGlone was in buoyant mood. He said: 'The feeling among the growing number of disgruntled fans is getting angrier. I firmly believe we will soon have to hire the Scottish Exhibition Centre to accommodate the army which is now behind us. If the board continue to dismiss us as a minority then on their heads be it. The rebel

135

consortium's bid of £18 million for change didn't shift them but we can and we will.'

What few people were aware of was the emergence of another millionaire on the scene. Gerald Weisfeld, who with his wife sold the What Everyone Wants store chain for more than £35 million, had always had an interest in Celtic. It was generated more through his stepson, Michael McDonald, than his own love of the team, but he had previously mentioned his interest. With the rebel consortium appearing to disappear, Weisfeld's interest was kindled again. At the EGM his stepson and city businessman Willie Haughey had spoken about a new move. Haughey had then offered the pact of five directors £300 each for their shares. The idea was that he would buy them out for £3.6 million which would open the door for a new board. Haughey, of course, had Weisfeld cash promised as back-up to make his offer possible. At the time it was regarded as a bit of a joke. But now the five directors had been contacted again. The offer, it seemed, was genuine.

One man was very interested . . . Celtic director David Smith. He noted the offer and the fact it was still, apparently, on the table. Smith contacted the other four members of the pact and reminded them the offer was still there.

It was on a cold and bleak Saturday in December that Smith arranged a meeting at Grant's house in Cumbernauld before heading for the game against Dundee. It was a meeting Grant remembers well. He recalled: 'The Weisfeld deal, which had been done through David Smith, was put on the table. I'm not sure what kind of involvement Chris or Michael had in it. Michael claimed he had none. Chris very little. All the negotiations were done through David Smith. Smith told us at that meeting that he could only see the offer of £300 a share from Weisfeld and that was the one option, the only one at that time, that he thought was the most favourable. Obviously it was discussed and we decided that if something could be pieced together with Cambuslang and then a public share issue sought that would be a more acceptable option to selling out to Weisfeld. The intention then was to get money into the club and open it out to the punters at large and make Cambuslang happen. Smith then said he would go away and try and make all of that happen. But the weeks passed and nothing really happened.

'Fergus's plan had looked good in parts but maybe he had been badly advised on some of it. I met with Fergus I don't know how many times and I said to him I didn't think all of his plan was realistic and there were things that should be changed. He told me if I thought that was the case then tell him and he would come and discuss them with the board. But nobody was really willing to discuss it with him. At least David wouldn't and Chris wouldn't. Michael, though, was always willing to talk, to be fair to him, but it needed the board. David Smith claimed that the only time he would meet him was from a position of strength, once we had won the contest and that was all he saw it as, a contest. He simply saw it as something you won or lost and if you won it you went to the opposition in a position of strength with your proposals. We had won the EGM but Fergus had gone.'

Christmas was fast approaching and it looked like being another one lacking in peace and goodwill to all men who had Celtic board connections. The bank had also been leaning rather heavily on the club but only Smith and fellow director Chris White knew about that. The others appeared to be more than a little in the dark. Celtic had tried to tell shareholders the annual accounts were looking better. But in reality the profit-and-loss account showed combined losses of more than £6 million and the balance sheet showed debts of £7.2million. The bottom line was Celtic Football Club was, on paper, only worth £571,309.

In addition, there were two main aspects of the accounts which worried rebel financier David Low. The club's accountants insisted on one figure being mentioned as it was not included in the club's statements due to what the accountants referred to as: 'qualified opinion arising from disagreement about accounting treatment'. It amounted to £122,374 and the accountants believed it should have been included as it effectively understated Celtic's losses. The second figure referred to other debtors and showed £431,000 for new stadium development. That was the amount paid to consultants *Superstadia* for the Cambuslang project. The amount had been put in such a way as to suggest it would be recouped at a later date. If the two figures were added together they would come very close to the total value of Celtic as stated on the balance sheet. There had also been no provision made for the amount of compensation expected to be paid to former chief executive Terry Cassidy, all of which meant the club was close to insolvency.

New Year brought little cheer to the club. In fact it got off to the worst possible start with a 4–2 thrashing from Rangers at Celtic Park on New Year's Day. Then it was revealed that the man Celtic had pinned their hopes on to raise cash for the Canbuslang 'dream' stadium – Pat Nally – had approached Brian Dempsey for investment. Nally's firm, Stadivarious, had made contact with Dempsey through a third party. It was an embarrassing blow to Celtic and the directors. Chairman Kevin Kelly had just declared a few days earlier that an announcement on the clinching of funds for Cambuslang was imminent. Kelly seemed to be the only one who thought so. At his cousin and fellow director Michael Kelly's office, the official club spokesman said: 'No firm date has been set for an announcement. If Kevin has a better idea than I have, and I doubt it, then by all means ask him.'

Damning words indeed, thought Dempsey, who had

said: 'An informal approach regarding investment was made but it has gone no further than that.' The Celts for Change group had now stepped up a gear and were behind a full boycott of a Celtic Park match. The official Supporters Association refused to join them but the other rebel band of Affiliation members were to be given the option of a boycott or to leave on the one-hour mark of a game as a show of protest. The Association said it would take a change in their constitution to boycott any Celtic game and that could only be brought about at the annual general meeting. But they agreed with the Affiliation to meet the Celts for Change group to discuss 'any common ground'.

Team boss Lou Macari was also feeling the strain. On 10 January, an hour after Celtic had lost to Partick Thistle at Firhill for the first time in 17 years, the manager finally came out of the dressing-room to meet the Press. Such a delay normally means the conversation will be short, bitter and to the point. But Macari chose the opportunity to take a swipe at the lack of cash available to him for new players and the apparent inaction by the board. He blasted: 'There is only one solution to this club's problems on the park and that is the signing of new players.

'We have no competition for places. We have no pace and we have no strength.

'This club is not on the right road and there is no point in me attempting to kid people that we are heading in the right direction.

'There are 35,000 Celtic fans who can see what this team needs on the park. I surely do not have to tell seven directors what that is, do I?'

Another defeat followed, this time at the hands of Motherwell. A week later, on 19 January, Macari decided he had had enough and plunged head first into the whirlwind which was creating havoc among his players. He had already met McGlone and his committee just after the defeat by Rangers at New Year. At that time he said he would try to arrange another meeting but with the directors and the other two supporters' groups present this time around. Now was the time. The manager was already feeling the strain from the players and did not want it to continue. His role as peacemaker was confirmed by McGlone who told the media: 'He wants us to attend a meeting between himself and directors before the match against Aberdeen tonight. Hopefully we will meet as many of them as possible, as most should be at the ground for the match. Obviously we would prefer it was Michael Kelly and Chris White, but we will have to wait and see.' The Association were the first group to pull out, saying they already had another meeting planned. Then it transpired only Tom Grant and Jimmy Farrell were considering the offer to attend. Mike Stanger, spokesman at Michael Kelly's PR firm, said his boss, along with directors Kevin Kelly, Chris White and David Smith, would not be attending. Macari had been snubbed. His peace bid had failed before it had begun. Only Tom Grant attended the meeting and a grim-faced McGlone said after it: 'There has been enough talking. Lou has tried and failed and risked a fall-out with the board over it. The talk is finished. It is time for action.'

The fact that Celtic only managed a draw against Aberdeen did not help. It was the team's first point in four matches but it merely highlighted the fact that all was not well. The game against Kilmarnock on 26 February was targeted by Celts for Change for the boycott. And the group warned it would result in an attendance of less than 10,000 at Celtic Park. That would be one of the club's lowest ever crowd figures and would hurt the club hard financially. McGlone said: 'I am confident enough supporters will use this match to show how they feel. But we are not bringing the club to its knees as some have suggested. The club is already on its knees.'

The besieged directors may have thought they had enough on their plate to worry about but, as the saying goes, it never rains but it pours. The long-awaited court confrontation with their former chief executive Terry Cassidy began at Glasgow Sheriff Court. Chris White turned up in court looking a confident man. David Smith and Jimmy Farrell were in court to witness the performance of their club secretary. A handful of supporters also sat in the public area but it was the constantly changing faces of court solicitors who appeared more interested. They popped in and out of the court between their own cases.

White was calm and collected in the witness box as he was led through his evidence by counsel for the club. Within minutes there was criticism of the former chief executive as White slated the financial dealings of Cassidy. He also revealed other problems which he claimed had led to Cassidy breaching his contract and ultimately losing his job. White spoke at length about a reception at Hampden Park on the eve of a Skol Cup final. Cassidy had not been invited but breezed in and, when told he shouldn't be there, referred to the Celtic directors as 'a bunch of women'. White then said Cassidy had given a television interview when previously instructed not to. He also tried to have letters printed in the *Celtic View* which criticised the manager and players. And, according to White, the former chief executive had failed to 'keep his finger on the financial pulse'. He referred to the decision to co-opt David Smith on to the board just a year after Cassidy's appointment, saying: 'The board felt it needed the business acumen of such a person.' Asked what Cassidy's attitude was to the appointment, White replied: 'I understood he felt threatened.' He said Smith soon expressed worries over the cash flow and thought Cassidy didn't have his finger on the pulse with regard to costs and income. White continued to criticise Cassidy for another day.

But things then changed when he was cross-examined by counsel for Cassidy. He quizzed him about Celtic's family dynasty then questioned White – a qualified accountant – over his paid job as club secretary. He asked him whether Celtic needed someone of his qualification to carry out work on a full-time basis which could be done by a clerk. White was not amused and said he didn't think it was a clerk's job. The grilling went on for another two days with White becoming increasingly nervous. He began to fidget and stutter as Cassidy's case was pushed home and the club's stance gradually looked more and more shaky.

But the time set aside for the case ran out and more court time had to be set for April. White and Smith could relax a little once again and, more importantly, no money had to be paid out. White left the court buildings looking visibly relieved.

But the problems facing him and his fellow directors were still piling up. Before he had time to draw breath, Rangers chairman David Murray slapped a sensational ban on Celtic fans. He said Celtic would get no allocation of tickets for any matches at Ibrox stadium unless the club paid for damage caused to seats during previous visits. Rangers had been in touch with Celtic for some considerable time over the issue but the directors at Parkhead had refused to pay up. They had never believed Murray would call their bluff and ban their supporters from Ibrox.

Celtic Chairman Kevin Kelly was unsure how to respond. He mulled the matter over before calling other directors and seeking their advice. He decided to speak out and claimed Rangers had ignored approaches to discuss vandalism at matches. He also suggested the absence of any arrests at the Celtic end of the stadium meant Rangers were not properly stewarding the fans. Rangers countered, denying the allegations and said the ban stood.

The move further infuriated Celtic fans who now saw their directors refusing to pay out around £20,000 for the damage and unable to negotiate a compromise. That anger grew three days later when Motherwell handed Celtic a third-round Scottish Cup defeat. The result effectively ended the season prematurely for Celtic. Yet the under-fire board of directors still denied the manager any cash for new players. After the game was over committee members of the official Celtic Supporters Association met with directors Kevin Kelly, Tom Grant and Chris White. The directors were asked if they had been offered cash for their shares and confirmed they had. The committee men – led by Chairman Jim Brodie – told the board how unhappy they were with things at Celtic and expressed concern for the future. The directors merely noted their concerns and tried to convince them things were going to improve.

The next day the Association held a delegates' meeting. More than 150 delegates from branches throughout Scotland packed into a school hall for the debate. They were angry men and they made their anger known to Association officials. Until then, the Association had been reluctant to take any action since tabling a vote of no confidence in the board. Now they demanded the directors quit and quit now. Association chairman Jim Brodie was not happy with that decision but he had to accept it. Delegates then wanted to discuss joining the boycott planned by the Celts for Change group. Brodie would have none of it. He rose to his feet and his face turned red as he got involved in furious exchanges with delegates. He threatened several times to close the meeting and ended up telling delegates to 'shut up'. But this outburst was met with a question from one man who shouted: 'Are you happy with the situation at Parkhead?'

Brodie blasted back: 'You must be joking. I am pig sick. I have been a supporter for 40 years and I believe a man of 80 could put the jersey on and do a better job.'

But delegates were in no mood to be subdued by talk. They wanted greater action by the Association. One stood up and shouted: 'We don't need you to back a boycott: we

143

will just stop running buses on the day.' He and others stormed out of the meeting.

Gerald Weisfeld was on holiday in Australia but he was still pulling the strings over the offer to the pact of five. In Glasgow Willie Haughey was in touch with the directors, hoping to conclude the deal in Weisfeld's absence. He was so confident of success that he was now talking openly with the media about the deal. He had also said he would like to talk to Dempsey and McCann about their possible involvement.

Dempsey was enjoying a holiday in the West Indies when he heard of Haughey's comments during a call to the office. In Arizona McCann had just returned home after another round of golf on a beautiful morning when the telephone rang. He had a long conversation with Dempsey. McCann was not happy at the thought of Weisfeld getting control and he agreed it was time for Dempsey and himself to make another move. He also decided to put the Weisfeld and Haughey offer firmly in its place. A conversation with a journalist in Glasgow soon made his views clear. McCann described the Weisfeld and Haughey bid as 'crazy'. He said: 'By offering £300 a share for shares which the board only value at £3 is ridiculous. This offer effectively makes it impossible for new capital to be brought in via a new share issue. And it is unlikely the consortium paying this amount for shares to oust the present directors will want to devalue their own investment by reducing the price. The only other way is for Weisfeld to pile in his own fortune. But I don't think he will want to bail out Celtic to the tune of £15 million, which is what it would take. I do not want to be any part of this deal, especially when it means lining the pockets of the five directors. For Haughey to suggest I would be interested is as crazy as his bid! This deal stinks. It is bad for the club and would be a shoestring job. Maybe this group have stars in their eyes but I believe the bid will stop dead once an audit is done on Celtic. The writing is on the wall and David Smith is trying to get the best possible price knowing the bank is about to knock on the door. If the bank comes to me and say listen, here's a deal, then I'll talk to them. Meanwhile I'm staying here and playing golf.'

Three days later Dempsey boarded a plane and headed for America as his family headed back to Glasgow. He had to sit down and talk face-to-face with McCann. Something was going to have to give at Celtic Park and they had better be prepared for it.

Chapter Thirteen

Return Leg

Wednesday, 23 February 1994.
Glasgow, 10 am.

THEY arrived one by one and climbed the steps to the first-floor city-centre office.

Steps they had climbed hundreds of times before. But this time was different. With each step the weight of Celtic Football Club bore down on them. The pressures had grown to massive proportions over the past few weeks and it was beginning to tell.

Michael Kelly looked drawn and tired. Tom Grant was pale and staring. Kevin Kelly seemed almost frightened to look anywhere but straight ahead. David Smith sat with his head on a hand, looking deep in thought.

Only Chris White appeared composed and alert, but his constant fidgeting suggested otherwise.

There was only one issue on the agenda in the offices of Desmond White and Arbuckle and it concerned the offer from the Gerald Weisfeld consortium including stepson Michael McDonald, businessman Willie Haughey and publican Paul Waterson. A lot of talking had already been done but nothing had been agreed. The debate was always hard, at times loud, and usually inconclusive.

The fifth member of the now infamous pact, David Smith, had urged the others to sit down again and consider the deal. It made sense to him, but then again it would. He was financially minded and realised the bank would not tolerate the situation at Parkhead for much longer. He was also a single man and the only one of the five who had invested a considerable amount of his own cash in shares. The rest, of course, had either inherited theirs or bought them cheaply.

White was now all for taking the £300-a-share offer and Michael Kelly looked set to follow. But Chairman Kevin Kelly and Grant were the only two still resisting. They still believed there was a way to save the club without having to jump ship. What about Smith's previous brief to look again at additional funding through new shares and to pursue the consultants over the promised cash backing for Cambuslang? Grant merely asked himself the question. It had all been said before and the lack of response was becoming boring.

As they talked and argued once more, fresh moves were being made by the rebel groups to bring to an end the farce which Celtic Football Club had become. Shareholders backing McCann and Dempsey officially launched their bid for another EGM to be held. It would allow the rebels to offer their package again but this time with the club under greater financial pressure from the Bank of Scotland.

But the big threat to that now was the Weisfeld offer, and Grant knew it. He remembered the meeting well. 'David Smith quite simply said, "I can't put this Cambuslang deal together. I might in time but I can't right now." He said we should consider taking the Weisfeld money.

'Kevin and I had already been meeting with Brian Dempsey and others. I was meeting with him, David Low,

Jimmy Farrell, others . . . I think I was meeting them almost hourly. At our meetings we hopefully talked through all the scenarios that were possible . . . if Weisfeld did this, if Weisfeld did that, if the board did this, if the board did that, and I think, quite accurately, we summed up all the possible eventualities.

'We reckoned that David Smith had already agreed to sign over his shareholding within the pact to Weisfeld. Kevin and I hadn't been any part of that. We decided that, if Fergus supported us financially, then we could destroy Smith. There were a number of calls made to Fergus to advise him of the situation. The pact was constructed in such a way that the five members had the first rights to buy the others' shares. You actually only had to buy control, you didn't have to buy all of them which would have been an even more painful episode for them. So Fergus basically guaranteed us that, if we stood up to them at that time, he would supply the financial backing to take out their shares. We were effectively the only people who could do it because they were going to sell to Weisfeld, not to Fergus. They had to offer to Kevin and me first.

'David Smith was quite broken at this time. He had had enough. Michael was always saying he didn't really want to sell his shares but he didn't see anything else happening and had to think of his other family members. So he effectively was ready to sell.

'So at that meeting of the five of us we talked it through so clearly. Our wording was so specific. We told them if that was the case, that they wanted to sell their shares, then Kevin and I would exercise all or part of our rights to purchase them. The "part of" wording was the all-important bit and the others knew it.

'That was the first opportunity we had to control them. So that really, if you like, put a spanner in the works. They couldn't deliver their shares to Weisfeld as promised. There were stories that Haughey had already been going about town saying he would soon be a director. Staff at Celtic Park were phoned and told to give them good service in the restaurant because they would soon be in control. Now David Smith and Chris and Michael could not sell out to them.'

McCann, meanwhile, was furious at the pressure Smith had apparently been putting on his fellow directors. From his Arizona home he called for Smith's resignation. McCann blasted Smith for trying to put the other directors under pressure to accept the £300-a-share offer. He said: 'If I was Kevin Kelly I would demand the immediate resignation of David Smith. As far as I can see he has effectively tried to twist the arms of the other directors into accepting this deal – a deal which is bad for the club. He made a big mistake getting into bed with these people and now he has been manacled by the pact.'

McCann also dismissed another link between him and the Weisfeld consortium. Reports that they wanted to talk with him were dismissed in the now usual way: 'I am told Weisfeld and Haughey want to talk to me. Big deal. I will not be party to paying these directors any money. The only people I will talk to now are the Bank of Scoland. They are Celtic FC now.'

Matt McGlone had been watching the exchanges and felt it was time the fans became involved in this latest development. Celts for Change then invited Haughey and McDonald to a meeting to explain their proposed plans for the club. McGlone said: 'There are a lot of questions which remain unanswered, like what additional cash will be invested if the directors are bought and where will it come from? We want to know how they propose to reduce the debt, what their stadium plans are and those for the manager and team. So far there has been silence on these issues and that is not encouraging.'

And the silence remained.

Haughey and McDonald both failed to appear at the

Celts for Change rally in the City Halls. It was the group's biggest and most emotive meeting yet. Despite the absence of Haughey and McDonald the meeting exploded in euphoria as Brian Dempsey turned up. He was not expecting to make a speech but he did. It was moving, powerful and poignant and had the 1,400 capacity audience cheering. Dempsey told them he saw a situation where the Bank of Scotland would step in 'within weeks' and finally bring an end to the board. It so moved one fan that he got to his feet, approached the microphone in front of the stage and, with tears in his eyes, said: 'Thank you, Mr Dempsey. There is a lot of feeling over this. Y'know, I'm glad my faither's deid, 'cause if he were alive all this wi' the board would've killed him.' It was that kind of night. Afterwards the crowd refused to leave until they had finished singing. For McGlone and the rest of the Celts for Change committee – Brendan Sweeney, David Cunningham and Colin Duncan – it was the greatest night of their group's short life.

But the next morning the stark reality was still with them – and so were the directors of the board at Celtic. By now the directors had reached total stalemate with the coup by Kevin Kelly and Tom Grant blocking the sale of shares to Weisfeld who, from Australia, had sent a message of hope for the changes he wanted to make.

Grant knew a move had to be made by the others and he was right. He recalled: 'It got to the point where David Smith had to come back with something else. All the negotiations were done through Smith. My contact regarding the Weisfeld deal had been Willie Haughey who kept me well informed until the last month, then all contact was severed. The last thing I remember him saying to me is the offer of £300-a-share is on the table so long as all seven directors resign. I told him it would not be on the table for me because I would not resign under those circumstances.

'At that point David Smith became more of a player. We all, the pact, met again and he went back to the Cambuslang project. He asked that if he could finish that off, present it with the relevant backing, would we agree to that? He said shares could be sold to the supporters, money raised and it would be a better idea than selling out to one particular individual. It was obvious to us all at that stage that this particular board would have to go in its entirety. We had no credibility. So we would have to change the board and the idea would be to form a public limited company which would have a board with none of the current directors on it. That board would run the company and the Cambuslang stadium. We would also have a board for the football side of things which maybe two or three or four of us could be on. If we did that, Smith would go.

'Smith became increasingly difficult to get hold of but I saw him at Celtic Park and he had now arranged a new conference to tell the media that Cambuslang was still on, in fact, was progressing. I asked him if he was serious about reviving Cambuslang. I suggested it was pie in the sky. But he said no, he had guarantees, the funding was in place. I told him I would only back him if and when the guarantees were there. Chris White believed him but I think even Michael doubted whether he could pull it off. Smith insisted he had these guarantees. You had to think that a guy like him would not put his credibility on the line if he didn't have those guarantees in writing.'

The pact of five directors agreed to the news conference – the other two, Jimmy Farrell and Jack McGinn, were not informed. On the evening of 24 February, the club put out a note to the media informing them of a news conference the following morning. The press thought it could be only one thing . . . the board were resigning. But, if that were the case, Dempsey knew nothing about it. Did that mean he had lost? The media circus duly turned up at Celtic Park. They crowded into the stadium and waited excitedly.

Michael Kelly, Grant and White sat in a middle row of seats. Chairman Kevin Kelly then marched in with consultant Pat Nally behind him and Smith bringing up the rear.

The conference was orchestrated by Smith and newsmen and sports writers sat in disbelief as Smith spoke about Celtic's twenty-first-century vision. This was effectively the same Cambuslang 'dream' announced two years before and which had still to see the light of day even through full planning permission. Smith told the assembled mass that there would be the stadium with £20m already in place. The underwriting for the funding had been agreed with international merchant bank Gefinor. And a new company would be formed with a new 25,000-share issue raising £6 million. The club would go public with a stock-exchange listing by the end of the year, and a new and separate board – Celtic plc – would be formed to run Cambuslang. He also said the pact of five would be disbanded to allow the directors to be replaced, at least in part.

Smith said: 'These proposals transcend past and present factions and family interests and will provide supporters and financial backers with a completely new concept of how a football club should be run in the modern world. This is a comprehensive and visionary package of radical measures designed to take the club into a glittering new future.'

'Astounded,' was how Willie Haughey reacted to the news.

'Stunned,' was the reaction from Matt McGlone.

'Fiasco' was how Brian Dempsey described it.

Smith had also used the opportunity to claim that he was not aware of any director who had sought a buyer for his current shareholding, saying: 'All of the major shareholders would rather see all available funds invested in Celtic.' It immediately led to Weisfeld and Haughey withdrawing their offer of £300 a share, with Haughey accusing Smith of betrayal. They said they would now offer their help to McCann and Dempsey. Dempsey simply dismissed the whole thing as 'a nonsense'. Even director Jimmy Farrell, who learned of the news from the media, claimed the proposals would only 'serve to prolong the continuing agony'. McGlone promised the proposed match boycott would go ahead.

Team boss Lou Macari was one of the few who thought the announcement was 'a step in the right direction'. This statement confused even top striker Charlie Nicholas. The unofficial spokesman for the players added: 'I will have to go away and digest all of this.' He did and after the announcement he and several other prominent players decided to take action. They requested a meeting with Dempsey and Haughey who were now talking about a possible joint approach to fight the board. Nicholas recalled: 'Myself, Packie Bonner and Paul McStay met them. It was initially arranged through Paul McStay after the announcement of the rebirth of Cambuslang. We all thought enough was enough and it was time to say something. We had thought about putting in transfer requests. With Peter Grant we would have gone to the other players to ask their opinion because feelings were now strong in the dressing-room that we had had enough. You were probably looking at about eight or nine players in that dressing-room who had been brought up with Celtic so we were more inclined to get involved. The whole thing was separating the board, the players and the fans. David Smith had announced all of this and I had never even been introduced to the man in all the time he was here. He never said hello to anyone or introduced himself to the players. He flew up for games and went away again. We had no contact with this man whatsoever and there was no effort made by the other directors to introduce him. He appeared out of the blue, and towards the end we realised

153

he was obviously running the ship. We thought something needed to be done but it was put kindly and in a nice manner by Brian Dempsey that it wouldn't be necessary and that time would take its course. We accepted that but still wondered about the announcement and where the money was coming from.'

They were not alone, thought Dempsey. Who was Gefinor? The international merchant bank said by Nally and Smith to be providing the £20 million cornerstone funding for Cambuslang is based in the Cayman Islands and has connections in Libya. But little else was known about it. Scottish financial experts knew nothing of it. The questions were now coming in thick and fast.

Gefinor Finance UK Ltd proved to be the UK wing of the offshore finance house based in Grand Cayman. According to the Bankers Almanac, Gefinor has a Cayman Islands category I practising certificate which allows it to practise abroad but not in the Cayman Islands. It is not registered with the Bank of England as a bank allowed to practise in this country, nor is it listed with the Securities and Futures Authority as a stockbroker. It was registered by another financial watchdog, the Investment Management Regulatory Organisation (IMRO), but had resigned.

Michael Kelly's office released a statement claiming Gefinor was a leading and respected international merchant bank. And he pleaded with shareholders to give the club their full backing for the new plans. Kelly said: 'People need to focus on the proposals themselves. If they go through them one by one they must agree they are good for Celtic. We propose a new stadium at Cambuslang, the pact of five to be disbanded and supporters allowed to put money into their club. It is up to people who agree all these things are good for Celtic to explain why they would vote against them. I really don't see any good reason to.'

Dempsey responded and dismissed Kelly's claims as 'Kidology'. He added: 'Nothing changes. If the current board are willing to resign then they should do so now, not in six months time. We believe it is their intention to remain on any new board.'

Kelly replied: 'I am committed to seeing the whole of this plan through until the share flotation. That is the time when the board will stand down.'

There was only one small problem with his optimism. Gefinor.

Chapter 14

The Final Whistle

Monday, 28 February 1994.
Newsroom, *Evening Times*, Glasgow, 8.00 am.

THE weekend had been one long Celtic story and more doubts had been cast over Friday's announcements. News editor Robbie Wallace was wondering what the next development would be.

Geneva was an hour ahead of British time and as the clock ticked on, the reporter making the call was sitting looking at the bank's name. Gefinor – what a strange name, he thought. He wrote the name down and started re-arranging the letters. It was the sort of thing anyone who indulges in crosswords or word games tends to do. Mix the letters about and see what other names you can come up with. Ronfige, fignore . . . or how about f-o-r-e-i-g-n.

Sounded good. A nice twist to the tale. A little known merchant bank from overseas called Gefinor – an anagram of foreign.

It was now 9.30 am in Geneva and the call was made. The telephone rang in long, intermittent bursts. The girl answered in French to which the reporter responded. He was put through to the investment department.

The man who answered sounded local but his English was good. 'Celtic? Underwriting £20 million? I don't think so.'

It was the first indication something was seriously wrong. That intuition to check directly with the bank's headquarters immediately after the weekend had proved right.

The man in the investment department then transferred the call. David Hagen answered. He was an executive committee member of the bank – an American who was somewhat suspicious of the call. Why, he thought, should I be getting a call at this time in Geneva from a British newspaper. 'Celtic? £20 million? A new stadium in Glasgow, Scotland?' There was a pause before Hagen continued: 'Well, yes, I am aware of something but I have not personally seen a request for commitment. I do not think there has been. Look, to be quite frank, it is something you should be talking to our London office about. I do not want to say anything more. Edward Armaly is the man you want but he's in America and I'm afraid I don't have a number for you.'

At the small London offices of Gefinor it was once again an answering machine – the same answering machine as was heard on Friday when callers tried to get through. Again it was back to intuition. International directory enquiries found a listed number for Gefinor in New York. It was the obvious place to start. But if Armaly was there the timing had to be perfect. The call had to go through before Hagen's from Geneva. There was little doubt he would call and ask Armaly what was going on. Armaly might then clam up.

The call went through at one minute to nine am New York time. The telephonist was in sharp. Her accent was thick as she drawled: 'Mr Armaly? One moment.'

157

The transferred call was answered after a single ring: 'Edward Armaly.'

He'd been caught cold. Geneva had got to him first – by fax – and wanted to know what was going on but he had not expected this call. In a Lebanese accent he said: 'I'll tell you what happened and hope it is reported accurately.

'Stadivarious, this Nally man, talked to us several months ago and we said it could be an interesting project but we have not engaged ourselves with them. That's the whole story. We met some months back but nothing else has happened.

'It has not been pursued since then. We are not engaged. We are not in. We are a financial institution and it's not so easy to put a big amount of money in unless you know what the risk is. There has not been the input for us to know that.

'The proposal which came to us was not to support Celtic Football Club; it was to finance the construction of different stadia. We have nothing to do with Celtic Football Club. It is absolutely wrong of them to say we are putting up £20 million for a stadium in Glasgow for Celtic.'

There was no stopping Armaly now. He had committed himself and he was making damn sure the facts were reported. After all, he had the bank's reputation to protect. He also had his job to protect.

'We will not get involved in anything if there is one iota of risk. I am shocked they have said this.

'I am here in New York and read about this in newspaper clippings faxed to me by head office in Geneva. When I saw what they were saying I was very surprised. I know there's a lot of debt in Celtic as a club and they don't have the best flow to borrow £2 million let alone £20 million.

'We are prudent investors. There is obviously some misinformation on the market. We don't have any agreement either with Stadivarious or Patrick Nally.

Patrick Nally is a promoter. He merely told us about an opportunity but not about Celtic. We will not get involved in building a stadium with Celtic.

'It is unfortunate it has reached the stage where the club have so much indebtedness their actual place as a club is questionable. No one is going to go and fund a stadium and still have it owned by a club who have so much indebtedness. So please print the truth.'

George McKechnie, editor of the *Evening Times*, did not have a problem with that request. In fact, when news editor Robbie Wallace had finished briefing him on the story, McKechnie already had a good idea of how the front page would look. The only problem would be for Celtic and, thought McKechnie, Michael Kelly in particular.

McKechnie and Kelly were old friends from the Celtic director's days as Lord Provost of Glasgow. He had crossed swords with Kelly on many occasions but the two had been able to talk and talk candidly.

Kelly had committed himself to the Cambuslang project and had publicly backed the announcement regarding Gefinor. It might well be Kelly had been somewhat naive. It might well be he hadn't learned from previous Celtic board dealings.

McKechnie remembered the time, almost a year ago, when Michael Kelly had called him to the office. Kelly asked him if he could meet with him in the morning. McKechnie was heading for London in mid-morning and told him so.

'What plane?' Kelly had asked.

McKechnie paused before answering. 'Probably the 11.15 but I could make it the 12.15.' He agreed to meet Kelly in the airport departure lounge area.

Kelly had been a worried man. He was under severe pressure trying to cope with Celtic's public relations. He had to swallow his pride a bit but he wanted advice and McKechnie was the man who could give him it.

They talked away in a corner with McKechnie advising and pointing out failings. They also discussed several problems which had arisen and those which might. After an hour McKechnie wished him luck and set off for London.

It seemed a bit ironic now that Kelly had since featured prominently in the *Evening Times* trying to defend the failings of Celtic Football Club. Now he was doing so again – but for how much longer?

The next day the front page carried the simple but effective headline: 'WHAT £20 MILLION?' The shock disclosure blew apart the ambitious plans and left Smith's '21st century vision' lying in tatters.

And there was more. The paper was also able to reveal that consultant Nally – the man supposed to be behind the deal – was involved in a multi-million-dollar lawsuit being instigated by a firm in the United States concerning another soccer-related venture.

But it was the Gefinor news which shook the club and its directors. Dempsey was first to offer his views. He said it made a mockery of the Cambuslang announcement and added: 'This whole affair has been conducted in the most unprofessional way. I call on David Smith to immediately make the fullest public statement on this matter.'

Smith, of course, was not about to do that. Anyway, no-one could find him nor Patrick Nally. Once again the Celtic response was left to Michael Kelly's sidekick Mike Stanger. He said: 'The Gefinor situation appears to be linked directly with Patrick Nally on six stadia rather than just the Celtic one. The contract is with him. We understand Gefinor has committed £65 million to Superstadia who are our consultants.'

Oh really? A call back to Gefinor's David Hagen confirmed it was yet another 'no'. He said: 'I am not aware of any deal involving Superstadia either. I don't know how Celtic got my name, but I would just as soon they don't have it.' Michael Kelly himself at last decided to speak to the *Evening Times*. He said: 'The time in New York is not sufficiently advanced to speak to Gefinor's Mr Armaly. Our position is unchanged from Friday. Gefinor have provided finance for Cambuslang. Patrick Nally is meeting Mr Armaly in New York today. We have an agreement with Stadivarious and there is a signed deal between Stadivarious and Gefinor for £65 million for stadia.'

Asked if he had seen that agreement Kelly replied: 'No, I've not seen it.'

As the media tried unsuccessfully to contact Smith or Nally the fans pressed ahead with their boycott of Celtic Park that night. The game was against Kilmarnock and most of the stadium lay empty. The directors claimed a crowd of 10,882 and claimed the boycott was not a success and despite the low figure it had remained above the 10,000 mark. What they were not aware of was that the Celts for Change group had hired an independent market research company to count everyone entering the stadium. Their figure was only 8,225 which tallied with the official police estimate of around 9,000. The boycott had worked and had been a great success. It was another body blow for the board who were coming under increasing pressure to come clean over Cambuslang and resign.

The next day Michael Kelly's public relations appeared to be in desperate need of saving. He was now saying he was still waiting for answers when Nally returned from New York. It seemed Nally couldn't telephone him to let Celtic know how a meeting with Gefinor's Armaly, if it happened, had gone. Nally added: 'Don't worry, you'll be the first to know – after I find out.'

But it was becoming increasingly clear that no-one was going to find out anything different. Dempsey had been kept closely informed of events by Tom Grant. But not even the Celtic director knew much. Looking back now Grant said: 'Smith had put his reputation on the line over that. I don't know what went wrong. I don't know if we'll ever know. But the guarantees he said were in place were not in place. I think the whole thing was a sham and David Smith was involved.

'I called Dominic Keane on the morning of the Cambuslang announcement and faxed him a copy of the news release. As much as he thought it could be good, he didn't think there was a hope in hell of it happening.

'Jimmy Farrell and Jack McGinn had not been aware of the Press conference. We felt if we had told them, particularly Jimmy, it would have immediately become public knowledge. We all regretted that but that was the way it was.

'We went up for the Press conference and after it Chris and I came down and told the staff the details of it but there was obvious disbelief. Cambuslang again? was the usual expression. No one could believe in it.

'Then the Bank of Scotland became a player. On that same Friday afternoon we came back to Celtic Park for a board meeting which had been called to discuss the Cambuslang proposal. We said to Smith it all looked the part and hoped everything he had said that day was true. Again he showed us a letter.

'Then the club's bank manager, Rowland Mitchell, appeared at the meeting. I didn't know he was coming. When he walked into the room I thought it had been a very shrewd move by Smith to get the bank manager along to endorse the Cambuslang plan.

'He sat down and said that whilst he saw the Cambuslang proposal and the way it had been delivered had exciting prospects for the future, it didn't deal with the club's extreme current problem which is the club was cash starved and how were we going to deal with that.

'I was quite cutting and asked him why he was just telling us now how serious the problem was. He looked surprised and said that after discussions with Smith and

White we had all been given letters asking for personal guarantees to the tune of £100,000 and telling us the bank was concerned.

'I said I had seen a letter but not a personal one. I knew that others had. At that point Chris White went up to his office, got the letters and handed them out to the other directors. That was the first time we had seen those letters. This all went back to a meeting members of the pact had been asked to attend in Edinburgh when the tax implications of taking Weisfeld's money would be explained to us. Chris White had phoned me and asked me to go. I wouldn't be going to the meeting because I wasn't taking the money.

He said David insisted I was there. I told him to tell David to phone me. He pleaded with me to attend the meeting. He said if I didn't my shares would be worth nothing and he didn't know how long he could keep the bank at bay.

'I asked him who was putting the pressure on. Him, the bank or Weisfeld? He said it was himself. I told him I was not going. Kevin wasn't going to attend either. Michael wasn't sure but later called me back to say he wouldn't be going either.

'Later I learned Willie Haughey was at that meeting and I believe the purpose of it was to put so much pressure on us that we would have left those offices that night having signed some agreement to transfer the shares to Willie Haughey.

'At that point it was obvious David Smith was dealing with Weisfeld and the bank and that he was taking Chris White and Michael with him.

'I am sure the bank was being informed of the Weisfeld moves. They knew the situation with Weisfeld, David Smith knew the situation with Weisfeld but we didn't. And both knew of these letters of personal guarantees. Was double-dealing involved?

'The bank manager at the board meeting that day described the scene as bizarre. It was obvious to him that the rest of us didn't know what was going on.

'The next day we all got another letter from the bank but David Smith told us not to worry, he could deal with it. None of us could get hold of him on the Monday to see if he had taken care of it.

'Then the Gefinor story came out. It shocked us. We still couldn't get hold of David Smith and on the Wednesday I told the others it was now critical and Chris said to me: "Go and see if your friends can help."

'I called Dominic and we met with him, David Low and a few others. We decided there and then that if Fergus McCann was willing to back us we would immediately go to the bank manager and give him an alternative proposal.

Chairman Kevin Kelly had also called Brian Dempsey and they all met to stall the process of bringing to an end Celtic's 106-year-old control by family dynasties. Kevin Kelly, Grant, Low and Dominic Keane went to the bank the next day, Thursday. Grant recalled: 'We learned the bank manager had previously met with Weisfeld and later discovered that even that morning Weisfeld had already offered to cover the club's debt to save us going into receivership. But we told him the advantage of the Fergus McCann offer was it had the majority of the board behind it – myself, Kevin, Jack and Jimmy.

'Fergus also had a business plan to inject money into the club. In all my meetings with Willie Haughey at no time did he say there was even any money for the club from the Weisfeld offer. He only said there could be at some time in the future. There was money for the shareholders but not the club.

'We left the meeting, went back and spoke to Fergus and Brian. We had guaranteed the money would be in place by 12 noon on the Friday but the bank wanted £1 million on Thursday. Brian and John Keane took care of that. By this time David Smith was public-enemy number one. Chris White was lost, and Michael still had confidence in Smith.'

A board meeting was called by Kevin Kelly, Grant, Farrell and McGinn at the offices of Pannell Kerr Forster – McCann's advisors – at very short notice. Smith could not be contacted and therefore did not appear. Both White and Michael Kelly claimed they had not been given enough time to attend. The others guessed that might be the case and it certainly didn't hinder what they had to do now – remove Smith and White.

The four did just that. They stripped the two of all executive responsibilities and called on them to go. Michael Kelly was given a final chance to side with the four and invited to meet Grant at the same offices later that day. Grant said: 'When he arrived and I told him what we had done he expressed his shock and disgust over our actions. I basically told him I noted his objections but, tough. He still thought we had over-reacted and Smith could still turn the situation round but there was no evidence he could or that he was even trying.

'I asked Michael if he wanted to sell his shares because we would exercise our right to buy them. He said only if his family were also made the same offer. I refused. He left and we all agreed to call for his resignation as well.'

By Friday morning the news had filtered through to the media. All hell was breaking loose. McCann was on his way from Arizona. Weisfeld had already flown in from Australia. Smith reappeared, flying into Glasgow airport and claiming he had no intention of resigning. Fans were turning up in their hundreds at Celtic Park anticipating an historic announcement.

There was just one more board meeting to be convened to end it all. Victory was only a few hours away . . . or so they thought.

Dempsey was in his office. He had been answering Press calls all morning. From now on they would have to

165

speak to Cathy Brennan. She was able enough to handle the most insistent callers. Cathy, after all, had been used to that over the years as Dempsey's secretary. He had plenty of other things on his mind right now and McCann was due in his office any minute, having flown in half an hour ago. There was a lot to sort out. Dempsey knew the three directors would not just walk away. They would either fight the move or seek a pay-off.

McCann duly arrived. His bright, mustard-coloured jacket announced his arrival rather loudly. He joined Dempsey and a couple of advisors in the boardroom. McCann didn't like the idea that he might have to pay the directors to go. He had always said he would never line their pockets but it seemed he may have little alternative. They decided to wait until the directors held their own board meeting before deciding on the tactic to take.

McCann, fully briefed, then headed for the Bank of Scotland to agree a deal with them over the overdraft and continued support for the club.

Dempsey headed to Celtic Park. Outside around 200 fans had already gathered and were enjoying the glare of media attention. The cheers went up as the green-and-white-clad supporters converged on Dempsey as he stepped out from the car. He was given a welcome fit for a hero. He went inside to discover the directors were still meeting. He would have to wait a while. About another half a dozen 'consultant' types also arrived and congregated in the reception area.

All the directors were inside and had been for an hour or so. Different meetings had been taking place. Grant, in his room, sat behind his desk facing White, Michael Kelly and Smith. Grant recalled: 'Michael said he thought it was terrible that Chris White's letter asking for his resignation had been delivered to his home and been opened by his wife. She had seen it before he was aware of it. But I just said she shouldn't have opened it.

'In the case of Smith, his letter was faxed to his London office buy his secretary refused to accept it. She must have tried to push it back into the machine. She just did not want anything to do with it. But we eventually had got confirmation he had received it. Anyway, Michael was still on about the way Chris in particular had been treated over the issue.

'I just told him that was good coming from him, the way he tried to have me and Jimmy removed from the board before. I told him he had put us through months of torture so what he was saying now was not even a consideration.

'He then said, "So that's what all this is about, it's revenge," I just looked at him and told him it had nothing to do with revenge. It was the fact we had been sold Cambuslang on half-truths and downright misleading statements to the point where people felt totally deceived.

'I said the whole thing was over. It would finish that day. Their resignations would be sought that day and they would sell their shares to us and go.

'David Smith then said we should just disband the pact because it was obvious it had served its purpose. But he wasn't going to get us that way. Disbanding the pact was the last thing we wanted. That would have meant they would be free to sell their shares to Weisfeld.

'I actually stood up and said if they didn't mind I'd go and get some legal advice on that. As I opened the door Michael asked where I was going for a lawyer. Why didn't I just pick up the phone and call one for advice. I said to him: "Have you looked outside?" There were about half a dozen in the hallway outside my office! We had everybody there that morning because we were really going to put the three under the cosh. We were going to make sure that it was finished that day.

'The advice was as I thought and there was no way the pact was going to be disbanded at that point. At that stage

I think they were resigned to the fact it was the end of them. I don't think Chris ever opened his mouth at that meeting.'

The lawyers were then put into action to reach agreement with the three. The hours ticked by as the three negotiated separately to satisfy their own conditions and try and get the best deal. The directors tried several times to start a board meeting to conclude things and officially accept the resignations and share transfers. But each time there would be some sort of hiccup as one or another decided the offer made to him was not acceptable.

The day had drawn into night. Still the fans sang and danced outside. Eventually, around 10.30 pm, final agreement with all had been reached. The first thing to be done was accept the resignations then sign the cheques for the shares which were then transferred. Then came the moment to dissolve the pact. Grant was still very apprehensive. He said: 'I wouldn't sign the pact documents until every other signature was on them. I don't know what it was. I just felt I couldn't trust anyone any more. When the papers were put in front of me I just passed them on until everyone else had signed. Michael looked at me and said: "What's wrong, don't you trust me?" I said no.'

Once everyone had signed the battle was over and the war had been won. A few legalities would have to take place the following day but it was just a paper exercise. With McCann, Dempsey and the new 'team' in control at last, they held the news conference to announce the takeover had succeeded.

Dempsey was physically and mentally drained. After the news conference he walked downstairs. The fans were still there. It was now raining and most of them were soaked. But they were still chanting and singing. They wanted to hear from him that it was all over. A cheer went up as Dempsey appeared at the front doors. He announced: 'It is finally over. Everything has been signed and you have a new board in control headed by Fergus McCann.'

Many fans openly wept when they heard the words. The board is dead . . . long live the board.

They cheered and started singing again, then began to disband and make their way home to girlfriends – and boyfriends for the girls there – wives and families they had left behind so many hours ago.

The three directors, Smith, Michael Kelly and White, slipped away into the cold, wet darkness. They had been ousted and, thought Dempsey, felt humiliated. Just as he had done three-and-a-half years before.

Dempsey left feeling tired but elated and with his head held high. A new era was beginning for Celtic Football Club.

Epilogue

Extra Time

Tuesday, 8 March, 1994.
Celtic Park, 10 am.

FERGUS McCANN looked as happy as a cat which had just pinched the cream. He joked with the posse of newsmen and photographers as he posed behind his desk.

His office was that of former chief executive Terry Cassidy and overlooked the front entrance to Celtic Park. A mountain of 'good wishes' and 'congratulations' cards lay on his desk. He opened them and read comments like: 'Good luck, Fergus . . . can we have our bill paid now?'

'This one says he "looks forward to better things" but there's no cheque with it. And here's one saying, "Congratulations, I'd like to sell you something". Oh really?' joked McCann

It was his fourth full day in power at Parkhead and he had agreed to a photocall to allow happy snaps of him at his desk. He already had a four-man team of accountants going through every scrap of paper at Celtic Park to build an accurate audit and find out exactly what had been happening to the cash. But he was not saying anything about that at this time. He didn't mind telling the newsmen that the bank position was now secure, staff were in good spirits and he was keen to meet the players and the manager to give them all the encouragement he could.

But McCann was about to learn that not everything runs smoothly in a football club, particularly Celtic Football Club. After a week it became clear the audit had shown up more than just the £9 million in overdraft and debts. There were other figures emerging which told a different tale of how Celtic had, on occasion, been run. Excessive spending, irresponsible squandering of cash, particularly on players' contracts and wages, and some quite incredibly high expenses paid to directors. The amount of cash wasted on the entire Cambuslang project from inception through to consultancy fees and other payments was around £1 million. There were also other business contracts which had been drawn up on terms well below the level expected of a club like Celtic. Some could be considered actionable from a legal point of view. McCann would have liked to show what had been taking place but he couldn't speak about them publicly. He had signed a 'pact' of what amounted almost to secrecy with the three departed directors. That was part of the price he had to pay. That along with the cash he had to pay.

Those directors had received up to £250 a share to go. And that from a man who said 'not a dime would line their pockets' if he had his way.

Well, he didn't have his way. And he still wasn't having his way. The arguments with Dempsey were now becoming frequent. They were not seeing eye to eye on things. Not that they always had, but this time it was getting serious. The other day Dempsey had come into McCann's office to find him surrounded by 'advisors'. Public relations people and accountants. Dempsey had told him he didn't need all these people around him. He effectively gave McCann a mouthful in front of these people and said they were all costing money. Money which didn't have to be spent.

Dempsey, of course, may have been right. But his frankness was now causing a serious rift between the two.

Dempsey was also the man in the spotlight with the media. He was the 'People's Champion' and McCann was somewhat in his shadow. The 'People's Champion' had already refused a seat on the board, preferring to head for America on business and pleasure and leave McCann to get on with the job.

Trouble was, thought Dempsey, McCann wasn't getting on with things as quickly as had been hoped. It was becoming clear, even to McCann, that running a football club is far from easy. Especially when it is effectively a one-man show.

Dempsey was now saying nothing to the media. He wasn't quite refusing to accept calls but he was taking a back seat. McCann would be master of his own destiny.

Tom Grant was also still on the board along with Kevin Kelly, Jack McGinn and Jimmy Farrell. Many of the club's huge support didn't like that compromise. But it would have to be like that until board changes could be introduced.

Grant accepted some would dislike him remaining. He said: 'I think the criticism I am now getting is inevitable when you have had people fighting different causes. But I don't feel I have been two-faced over anything. I feel I have been caught in the middle. I don't accept I switched from one side to the other. I listened to every side. I didn't agree with Fergus's initial proposal and therefore voted against it. I still feel justified in signing the pact because it did bring partial stability at least.

'I still believe I have a part to play in making the current changes happen. To expect every one of the seven directors to have resigned is unrealistic regardless of how each of us is thought of. There has to be a bit of continuity. I'm sure through time all of us will go but I feel Jimmy and I have played an important part in this takeover.

'At one time being a director of Celtic Football Club was the be all and end all, the most important thing in my life. But I am astute enough to know there are other, more important, things to life. However, I do intend to stay in the meantime and help get the club back on a sound footing. In a few years time if I thought the club was nice and comfortable and I thought there was something else I wanted to get involved in then I would.'

The one bright aspect so far though, from McCann's point of view, was the EGM he had called to push through the changes he wanted. Weisfeld and his consortium were back on the scene and had agreed to back McCann. The resolutions changing the club's constitution and increasing the share issue to include the supporters were unanimously approved. The rebuilding of Celtic Park would now go ahead and around £21 million from shares would come into the club. A deal had been struck with Terry Cassidy costing the club around £50,000 less than he had claimed for. All was looking good. All, that is, for McCann and Weisfeld. Not so Dempsey.

As McCann posed for photographs with Weisfeld inside the Celtic lounge at the stadium after the EGM, Dempsey met the Press and posed for the photographers outside beside the stairs.

As Weisfeld prepared to leave McCann was asked if he would then pose with Dempsey. His reply was: 'I think you've had enough shots, gentlemen.'

Outside the lounge Dempsey wished McCann good luck. He was heading for America after all but would return.

Weisfeld already appeared to have his name on a board seat. Asked if he would expect to be offered a directorship on his return, Dempsey replied: 'I never expect anything.'

As he left Celtic Park Dempsey turned and looked back at the stadium. A new era was indeed dawning, he thought. But what will it bring? What would people expect? Expect? He laughed to himself. Never expect anything, particularly if it has anything to do with Celtic Football Club.